TRENDS IN EMPLOYMENT

IN THE SERVICE INDUSTRIES

NATIONAL BUREAU OF ECONOMIC RESEARCH

NUMBER 59, GENERAL SERIES

Trends in Employment
in the
Service Industries

BY GEORGE J. STIGLER
Columbia University

A STUDY BY THE
NATIONAL BUREAU OF ECONOMIC RESEARCH, NEW YORK

PUBLISHED BY
PRINCETON UNIVERSITY PRESS, PRINCETON
1956

Printed in the United States of America
by Princeton University Press, Princeton, New Jersey

The study upon which this volume and the previously issued reports as listed above are based was made possible by funds granted by The Maurice and Laura Falk Foundation of Pittsburgh. The Falk Foundation is not, however, the author, publisher, or proprietor of this publication, and is not to be understood as approving or disapproving by virtue of its grant any of the statements made or views expressed therein.

PREFACE

The National Bureau studies of employment and output first covered manufacturing, then mining, agriculture, and public utilities and transportation. The large remaining area, generally described as the service industries, has been partially surveyed in studies of government, trade, and, on a more modest scale, domestic service and education. This final essay deals with the service industries as a whole, and attempts to give some—although all too little—depth to the survey by dealing in more detail with selected industries.

I have profited by the suggestions of Harold Barger, David Blank, Solomon Fabricant, and Thor Hultgren. I must express my debt to Jack Farkas for performing most of the statistical work. The charts were drawn by H. Irving Forman.

GEORGE J. STIGLER

CONTENTS

TABLES

CHARTS

TRENDS IN EMPLOYMENT

IN THE SERVICE INDUSTRIES

CHAPTER 1

THE GROWTH OF THE SERVICE INDUSTRIES

ONE of the earliest studies of workingmen's family budgets was published in 1797 by Sir Frederic Morton Eden, when he issued the celebrated book *The State of the Poor*. The study was the product of his own sympathy and diligence, supplemented by the assistance of a few clergymen and the services for a year of a hired assistant. The budgets were not a "sample" in any desirable sense, and they are restricted chiefly to the poorest families, but still they shed much light on the contemporary standard of living.

In 1937 and 1938 another study was made of the budgets of English workingmen's families. The contrast with Eden's study is itself enough to reveal the vast changes wrought during the intervening century and a half. The Ministry of Labour was the sponsor; between 10,000 and 12,000 budgets (in each of four quarters) were collected; scientific sampling was employed in selecting the families; the families generally had incomes under £250 (the corresponding figure for Eden's study was about £50), and each family was paid 2s.; 6d. for each weekly record of its expenditures.

We boldly compare the findings of these two studies (Table 1).

TABLE 1
Percentage Composition of Expenditures of
English Working Families, 1794 and 1937-1938

CATEGORY	AGRICULTURAL WORKERS		NONAGRICULTURAL WORKERS	
	1794	*1937-1938*	*1794*	*1937-1938*
Housing	4.6	8.3	6.0	12.7
Food	74.5	48.4	73.9	40.1
(Grain)a	(46.2)	(9.7)	(36.2)	(6.3)
Clothing	9.0	9.1	5.0	9.5
Fuel and light	4.4	8.6	5.4	7.6
Miscellaneous	7.6	25.6	9.6	30.1
Total	100.1	100.0	99.9	100.0
Detail				
Number of families	60	1,491	26	8,905
Persons per family	5.9	3.79	6.2	3.77
Average annual expenditure	£39 11s.; 11d.	£150 11s.; 1½d.	£40 7s.; 4d.	£224 5s.; 8½d.

a Included in food.

Source: Sir Frederick Morton Eden, *The State of the Poor*, London, J. Davis, 1797, Vols. II-III, and *Ministry of Labour Gazette*, London, Ministry of Labour, December 1940, pp. 304-305, and January 1941, pp. 9-11.

To measure the full extent of the change in family expenditures over time we should probably compare the agricultural workers of 1794 with the nonagricultural workers of 1937-1938. We find food costs to have fallen enormously relative to total expenditures —from 74.5 to 40.1 per cent. All other categories of expenditure rose, although only slightly in the case of clothing. The really vast expansion, however, was in the category of "miscellaneous": in 1937-1938 it consisted of a variety of categories (household furnishings, 11.6 per cent of "miscellaneous"; tobacco, 9.9 per cent; insurance premiums, 9.3 per cent; travel, 8.8 per cent; health and unemployment insurance, 8.1 per cent; medical care, 6.5 per cent; entertainment, 5.4 per cent; union dues, 5.3 per cent) that were generally unimportant or wholly absent in 1794.

A similar comparison, more precise in its earlier data but covering less than half as long a period, can be made for this country (see Table 2). Again the outstanding changes are the great drop in the

TABLE 2

Average Income and Expenditures of Massachusetts Working
Families, 1874-1875, 1903, and 1935-1936

CATEGORY	1874-1875 (1)	1903 (2)	1935-1936 (3)
Income	$762	$685	$1,378
Expenditures	740	632	1,415
Surplus	22	53	−37
Rent	124	132	244
Food	423	258	485
Clothing, shoes, dry goods	104	83	127
Fuel	44	32	128
Other	45	126	431
	Percentage of Total Expenditure		
Rent	16.7	20.9	17.2
Food	57.2	40.8	34.3
Clothing, shoes, dry goods	14.2	13.1	9.0
Fuel	5.9	5.1	9.0
Other	6.1	19.9	30.5
Total	100.0	99.8	100.0
Families in sample	389	1,189	1,872
Persons per family	5.14	3.92	3.05

Column	Source
1	*Sixth Annual Report of Bureau of Statistics of Labor*, Wright and Potter, State Printers, 1875. Families 27, 56, 78, 184, 195, 257,

fraction of income spent upon food and the great rise in "other" expenditures.

Such comparisons offer strong support for Dr. Ernst Engel's law, which in one form states that the richer a society, the smaller the fraction of expenditures made on food. The widely separated budgets suggest also that this rise in income leads to a large expansion of amusements, medical service, personal care, and similar services.

An immense transformation of the workingman's way of life has taken place in the last 150 years. The near halving of the share of income devoted to food tells as fully as any single ratio can that economic progress in this period outstripped that of all the centuries which had preceded.

But the budgets do not reveal the full extent of man's shift from the basic material requisites—food, clothing, and shelter—to the endless variety of public and private services. The budgets do not show the great expansion of government services, and in fact catch only the small part that workingmen pay for in direct taxes. The budgets do not separate the share of commodity costs going for marketing services or for business services which are not purchased separately. Let us therefore turn to the industrial composition of the labor force, which provides for the modern period a comprehensive account of the rise of the service industries.

1. The Trend of the Service Industries

Our study of the trend of the service industries begins, as a matter of statistical necessity, with 1870: the earlier period probably merged smoothly into that we study, but we cannot measure it numerically. The growth of the service industries, as measured by their labor force, has been consistent but not steady (see Table 3). If we consider the whole labor force, the share in service indus-

---

Notes to Table 2 (continued)

258, and 385 are omitted because rent is included in board, or home is owned and no imputed rental is given.

2 *Eighteenth Annual Report of the Commissioner of Labor Statistics*, Dept. of Commerce and Labor, 1904.

3 *Family Expenditures in Seven New England Cities, 1935-36*, Bureau of Labor Statistics, Vol. II, 1941. Three city classes (less than 25,000; 25,000-100,000; over 100,000) are combined with the number of "operative and kindred workers" in Massachusetts cities of these sizes in 1940 as weights.

tries increased from one-fifth in 1870 to one-half in 1950, but shows decades of near stability (1870-1880, 1910-1920) followed by spurts. If we consider only the nonagricultural labor force,

TABLE 3

The Labor Force in the Service Industries, 1870-1950

| | | ABSOLUTE NUMBER (THOUSANDS) | | PER CENT IN SERVICE INDUSTRIES OF: | |
	Total[a]	Nonagricultural Industries	Service Industries[b]	Labor Force	Nonagricultural Labor Force
1870	12,780	6,350	2,450	19.2	38.6
1880	17,195	8,585	3,320	19.3	38.7
1890	23,570	13,580	5,200	22.1	38.3
1900	28,700	17,990	6,920	24.1	38.5
1910	36,130	24,790	9,770	27.0	39.4
1920	41,230	30,110	11,360	27.6	37.7
1930	47,255	37,075	17,190	36.4	46.4
1940	49,970[c]	40,970	20,130[c]	40.3	49.1
1950	58,460[c]	51,445	25,560[c]	43.7	49.7

a Excluding workers with unknown industrial classification.

b To facilitate comparison of 1950 figures on the service industries with earlier years the 1950 census data on these industries have been revised to conform with Solomon Fabricant's classification of the labor force in the service industries for 1870-1940. Solomon Fabricant, "The Changing Industrial Distribution of Gainful Workers," *Studies in Income and Wealth, Volume Eleven*, National Bureau of Economic Research, 1949, pp. 41-43.

c Including the estimated number of members of the armed forces in continental United States only. The census estimates that about 150,000 members of the armed forces were serving abroad in 1940 (see *Population—Special Reports*, Bureau of the Census, Series P-44, No. 12, June 12, 1944, p. 2n). In 1950 according to census estimates there were 301,595 members of the armed forces stationed outside the continental United States (see *Census of Population, 1950*, Bureau of the Census, Vol. II, Part 1, Table 35, p. 87).

Note: The figures for 1870-1940 are derived from Fabricant's estimates of the industrial distribution of gainful workers. See Fabricant, *op. cit.*, Table 2, p. 42. The 1950 data are derived from *Census of Population, 1950*, Vol. II, Part 1, Tables 50 and 130.

there was no upward trend in the share of workers in service industries between 1870 and 1920, but after that a large increase.[1]

When we turn to the general categories of service industries, we find an almost unbroken expansion of every sector except the one

[1] The use of the nonagricultural labor force as a base to measure the industrial composition of the labor force calls for more defense than it usually gets. Unless one is prepared to make some assumption such as that the movement of people away from farms is subject to a set of explanations separate from explanations for other occupational movements, or that the source of migrating laborers has a decisive effect upon their destination, the nonagricultural basis seems rather artificial.

that was largest in 1870, domestic service, which has steadily decreased from a fourteenth to less than a thirtieth of the labor force (Table 4). Even the decline of domestic service has been

TABLE 4

Labor Force in Service Industries as Per Cent of Total
and Nonagricultural Labor Force, 1870-1950

	Trade	Finance and Real Estate	Educa-tion	Other Professional Services and Amusements	Domestic Service	Personal Service	Govern-ment, n.e.c.
			1. Per Cent of Total Labor Force				
1870	6.14	.34	1.49	1.10	7.36	1.96	.78
1880	6.72	.37	1.92	1.10	6.28	2.09	.81
1890	7.74	.69	2.16	1.48	6.45	2.72	.81
1900	8.57	1.05	2.26	1.74	6.06	3.38	1.05
1910	9.33	1.44	2.49	2.13	5.95	4.21	1.49
1920	9.85	1.94	2.84	2.62	4.12	3.95	2.23
1930	13.10	3.11	3.45	3.64	5.40	5.29	2.39
1940	14.37	3.10	3.36	4.64	5.22	6.20	3.38
1950	16.43	3.33	3.57	5.42	2.96	6.38	5.62
			2. Per Cent of Nonagricultural Labor Force				
1870	12.38	.68	2.99	2.20	14.80	3.94	1.57
1880	13.45	.73	3.84	2.21	12.58	4.19	1.63
1890	13.44	1.20	3.76	2.58	11.19	4.71	1.40
1900	13.66	1.68	3.61	2.78	9.67	5.39	1.67
1910	13.59	2.10	3.63	3.11	8.67	6.13	2.18
1920	13.48	2.66	3.89	3.59	5.65	5.41	3.06
1930	16.70	3.96	4.40	4.64	6.88	6.74	3.05
1940	17.53	3.78	4.10	5.66	6.37	7.57	4.12
1950	18.68	3.79	4.06	6.16	3.36	7.25	6.38

n.e.c. = not elsewhere classified.
Source: Daniel Creamer, "Changes in the Industrial Composition of Manpower since the Civil War," *Studies in Income and Wealth, Volume Eleven*, National Bureau of Economic Research, 1949, Table 1, p. 47. Figures exclude "industry not specified."

chiefly relative to the labor force (which tripled over the period) and only after 1940 did the absolute number of servants decline.

The last two decades in education display the only other instance of even a moderate pause in the relative growth of the service industries. The share of the labor force employed in education paused in its upward trend as the birth rate fell from 1920 to 1935. The high level of births in recent years has transformed the age structure of the population: in 1940 the eighteen-year-olds were the most numerous age group (2.6 million); in 1950 it is the three-year-olds (3.6 million). We may expect a large further growth of employment in education.

With this temporary exception of education and the persistent exception of domestic service, the record has been one of substantially unbroken growth relative to the labor force. In general the service industries which were largest in 1870 have grown least rapidly, but even wholesale and retail trade, which had one-sixteenth of the labor force in 1870, has grown to one-sixth of the labor force. The number employed in trade now exceeds that in agriculture and mining combined, and is two-thirds of the number in manufacturing.

Government employment includes persons performing not only services that only governments supply, such as law enforcement, regulation, and national defense, but also services provided by nongovernment bodies as well (such as education and construction). Only the former employees ("not elsewhere classified," or n.e.c.) are reported separately in Table 4. This smaller group grew more rapidly than the total of all government employees, which we discuss later, because it excludes education, the largest peacetime function of government in the census years before 1950.

Of course the industry categories distinguished in Table 4 are broad: finance includes pawnbrokers and governors of the Federal Reserve System; professional services and amusement include judges and flagpole sitters; government, n.e.c., includes an astonishing variety of activities. If we could look beneath the aggregates—as we shall for certain industries in later chapters—we would find that the variety of patterns of growth was much greater than Table 4 suggests: there have been industries, such as drinking places, which have vanished from sight (or at least became less noticeable) and then reappeared; industries, such as nonprofit organizations and public insurance, which have grown from almost nothing to substantial size, and others, such as livery stables, which have followed the opposite and more painful course. This diversity of pattern is worth keeping in mind simply to discourage any belief that growth of employment in the service industries has been universal or is inevitable, or, for that matter, the belief that we are likely to find a single set of explanations for so diverse a group of industries.

Comparisons like those above which state that the number of persons in trade exceeds the number in agriculture and mining combined, or that the number in domestic service considerably exceeds that in railroading, are often criticized as exaggerating the importance of the service industries. In at least one sense such comparisons should be criticized, for a simple count of heads of workers is a poor measure of the importance of an industry to an economy. It is poor because it ignores the quality of the labor force: are the service industries staffed chiefly with relatively skilled or unskilled workers? It is a poor measure, also, because it ignores the quantities of the other productive resources cooperating with labor in production.

Both of these points may be illustrated, although only approximately and for only a few broad industry categories, from the national income data (Table 5). We may measure the quality of workers by their wage incomes, although we must recognize that our first method of estimating the wage incomes of professional workers (e.g. that of a physician by the average of his employees' wages) is seriously biased downward, and our second method (which includes entrepreneurial property incomes) is biased upward. It is apparent, however, that if we use an average of these earnings as a measure of labor quality, the service industries do not systematically have a smaller share of the labor force than when we count heads: only in personal and domestic service is the per cent of the total labor force much greater than the per cent of earnings, and in the professions the share in earnings is much higher. And when we shift to an "income originating" measure, which takes account of all forms of productive contributions including those of property, we find that the service industries again fall on both sides of the national average. In finance, insurance, and real estate the share of all income greatly exceeds the share of labor income; in personal services the opposite relationship is found in lesser degree.

The service industries are thus of roughly equal economic significance, whether measured by employment, labor earnings, or national income originating. There are other bases for ranking industries, some metaphysical and some capable of comprehensible interpretation.[2] But none, I suspect, justifies snobbishness toward the service industries.

2. The Public Economy

Although we shall discuss later certain service industries (the

[2] The most significant, I think, is that which measures the "importance" of an industry by its short-run indispensability (inelasticity of demand), for this measure is related to the political and monopolistic power the industry may achieve.

9

TABLE 5

Percentage Use of National Resources by Selected Service Industries, 1950

INDUSTRY	LABOR FORCE[a]	LABOR INCOME		INCOME ORIGINATING
		Wages and Salaries[b]	Wages and Salaries plus Income of Un-incorporated Enterprise[c]	
Trade	19.47	20.18	20.87	18.10
Wholesale	4.62	6.06	5.96	5.71
Retail	14.86	13.84	14.65	12.40
Finance, Insurance, and Real Estate	3.41	3.87	3.73	8.61
Insurance	1.41	1.63	1.58	1.38
Real Estate	.94	.82	.83	5.48
Service	13.30	9.87	10.58	9.48
Hotels	1.07	.78	.63	.55
Personal	2.05	1.55	1.51	1.19
Domestic	3.01	1.51	1.39	1.11
Motion Pictures	.40	.40	.39	.35
Other amusements	.49	.43	.39	.33
Medical	2.11	1.51	2.35	1.87
Legal	.38	.29	.70	.55
Engineering	.27	.37	.37	.30
Education (private)	.83	.65	.57	.47
Government	12.56	13.27	12.24	9.77

a Proprietors plus full-time equivalent employees.

b Includes entrepreneurial wage income estimated as number of proprietors times average annual earnings of full-time employees.

c Wages and salaries here are exclusive of estimated wage income of entrepreneurs. For industry subgroups the income of unincorporated enterprises was calculated by applying the ratios of 1949 income of unincorporated enterprises as reported respectively in the *National Income Supplement, 1954, Survey of Current Business* (Dept. of Commerce), and *Survey of Current Business*, July 1952, to the corresponding 1950 series in the *Survey of Current Business*, July 1952.

Source: *Survey of Current Business*, July 1952, Table 16, p. 19, and *National Income Supplement, 1954, Survey of Current Business*, Exhibit 2, p. 77, and Tables 13, 14, 25, 27, and 28.

military and college teaching professions) which are wholly or partly administered by governments, we shall not attempt to discuss in any detail the vast range of economic activities performed by modern governments. The reader is referred to Solomon Fabricant's recent work for such a discussion.[3] But it is desirable now to

3 Solomon Fabricant, *The Trend of Government Activity in the United States since 1900*, National Bureau of Economic Research, 1952.

take at least a glance at this group of activities, for they are chiefly in the category of services.

It is not quite accurate to say that all the important forms of government employment are service industries, and indeed our pervasive governments are represented in every broad industry category (see Table 6). But there is only one commodity-producing industry

TABLE 6

Government Employment by Industry, 1950

INDUSTRY	EMPLOYMENT Number (thousands)	Per cent	GOVERNMENT EMPLOYMENT AS PER CENT OF INDUSTRY EMPLOYMENT
Agriculture	21	.3	.3
Forestry and fisheries	25	.4	20.8
Mining	2	.0	.2
Construction	329	5.1	9.6
Manufacturing	130	2.0	.9
Transportation and public utilities	352	5.4	8.1
Street railways and buses	110	1.7	34.0
Utilities and sanitary services	194	3.0	24.8
Trade	29	.5	.3
Finance and real estate	57	.8	3.0
Business and personal services and entertainment	36	.6	.7
Professional services	2,021	31.1	45.3
Medical and health	446	6.9	27.4
Education	1,539	23.7	74.3
Public administration	3,485	53.6	100.0
Postal service	454	7.0	100.0
Federal public administration	1,009	15.5	100.0
State and Local public administration	1,025	15.8	100.0
Armed forces	997[a]	15.3	100.0
Industry not reported	17	.2	2.0
Total	6,504	100.0	11.4

[a] In the United States.

Source: *Census of Population, 1950*, Bureau of the Census, Vol. II, Part 1, Table 133.

(construction) in which government employment is appreciable relative to both total industry employment and total government employment. Government employment in the transportation and public utility industries is larger, and if we transferred the postal service to this area, as in consistency we should, this group of industries would contain a considerable part of government employment. But all the rest of government employment falls in service industries such as education and health, or in the public services *sui generis*. It should be remarked that if we were studying other countries this identification of government activity with service industries would clearly be illicit: in the United Kingdom, for example, 2.4 million workers (in a total labor force of 23 million) were in nationalized industries in 1950.[4]

Government employment has had scarcely any upward trend relative to the service industries, if it is not too naïvely optimistic to treat the spring of 1950 as possibly atypical of the future (Table 7). But the service industries themselves have in the aggregate

TABLE 7

The Labor Force in Service Industries and
in Government Employment, 1900-1950

| | LABOR FORCE (THOUSANDS) | | GOVERNMENT LABOR FORCE AS PER CENT OF SERVICE INDUSTRIES (3) |
	All Service Industries (1)	Government (2)	
1900	6,920	1,110	16.0
1910	9,770	1,736	17.8
1920	11,360	2,529	22.3
1930	17,190	3,206	18.7
1940	20,130	3,644a	18.1
1950	25,560	6,559a	25.8

a These figures were adjusted to 1930 base.

Column   Source
  1   Table 3.
  2   *1900-1940*: Solomon Fabricant, *The Trend of Government Activity in the United States since 1900*, National Bureau of Economic Research, 1952. *1950: Census of Population, 1950*, Bureau of the Census, Vol. II, Part 1, Tables 45, 118, and 133.

grown rapidly and without interruption, and our mode of presentation should not conceal the fact that the employees of governments grew sixfold in the half century, while the labor force only doubled.

Fabricant's study indicates that growth took place in all major and virtually all minor functions of government, and that one must look to trifling functions such as regulation of midwives in order to

[4] See Moses Abramovitz and Vera Eliasberg, *The Growth of Public Employment in Great Britain*, Princeton University Press for National Bureau of Economic Research, in press.

discover absolute declines in activity.[5] The generality of growth of government functions, however, is partly an organizational illusion: A given agency has a tendency to adapt itself to changing institutions. The same navy that once fought with wooden sailing vessels now fights with atomic submarines; the same Federal Communications Commission that once regulated only radio takes on the regulation of television in stride. If private industries were defined merely by function—say, transportation—rather than by both function and method of performing it—like railroads—we should also find declining private industries to be most uncommon in a growing economy.

Many individual functions of government have grown for exactly the same reasons that various private industries we discuss later have grown. As our population has become more urban, it has been almost inevitable that we should have more public employees to enforce traffic rules, watch the sanitary practices of consumer and businesses, teach children, and the like. As our population has become wealthier, it is natural that it should demand a better grade of bank or schoolhouse just as it demands better food and housing.

It is not possible to state precisely how much of the expansion of government economic activity we can explain by such traditional determinants of industry growth. One may conjecture, however, that much of the growth must be based upon different factors. Developments such as the rise of per capita income and the growth of cities characterized the whole nineteenth century, and yet the data seem to suggest that the growth of public employment was small relative to the labor force during this century.[6] A basic shift in attitudes toward individual and social action, or in the distribution of political power which has changed the effective importance of different attitudes, has probably been basic to much of the growth of government economic activity. We shall not undertake to investigate this large subject.

[5] Fabricant, *op. cit.*, p. 82.
[6] See Abramovitz and Eliasberg, *op. cit.*, and Fabricant, *op. cit.*, p. 14.

CHAPTER 2

A HISTORICAL PREFACE

WHEN we seek to explain the trends in employment in various service industries, we shall repeatedly encounter a particular set of influential economic developments. They can all be subsumed under the traditional headings of the theory of consumer demand: income, prices, and tastes. Normally the economist places primary weight on income and prices, and hopes that tastes have been reasonably stable.

In the study of long-run trends in consumption, however, this neglect of tastes is not desirable; and it is not necessary. Many influences upon "tastes," such as the characteristics of the population, are measurable and can profitably be brought to bear on the analysis of trends in consumption. The present chapter summarizes certain basic changes in "tastes," and also in income. These changes in tastes will be familiar to all readers, but it seems desirable to set them forth with some detail here rather than burden the discussions of individual industries which they have influenced.

1. Population

In 1950 our population was approximately five times as large as in 1860 (Chart 1). This fact alone suffices to explain the increase in the absolute number of workers in most broad industrial groups, but it does not aid us in explaining the differential movements in which we are especially interested.

The population of 1860 was essentially agricultural: 4 out of 5 persons lived in rural areas, and usually on farms. In 1950 only 2 out of 5 persons lived in rural areas, and less than 1 of these 2 lived on a farm (Table 8). The urbanization has taken place in almost a cyclical pattern: decades of rapid and of slow decline in the percentage of people in rural areas have alternated regularly except for the decade 1910 to 1920. The decades characterized by exceptionally long and severe depressions—the 1870's, the 1890's, and the 1930's—are those in which urbanization progressed most slowly.

The percentage of the population in rural areas has been falling at a slower average rate in recent decades. This retardation is to some extent inevitable in the arithmetic: a decline of roughly 40 percentage points from 1860 to 1950, if duplicated in the ninety

14

CHART 1

Population of the United States, 1860-1950, Total, under 15 Years of Age, and 60 Years of Age and Over

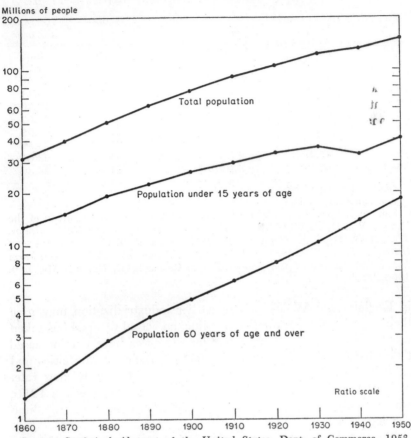

Source: *Statistical Abstract of the United States*, Dept. of Commerce, 1953, Tables and 21, and *Historical Statistics of the United States, 1789-1945*, Dept. of Commerce, 1949, Series B Tables 81-144.

years to 2040, would eliminate the farm and rural nonfarm population of the country. But it is due also to the relative increase of the rural nonfarm population: this part of the population has gained ground relative to the total population in the last forty years.

The urban population of 1860 lived usually in cities well under 100,000. Another striking development has been the relative growth of the largest cities. By 1920 half the urban population was in cities over 100,000. Here again retardation is evident; and

TABLE 8

Percentage Distribution of Rural and Urban Population, 1860-1950

| | | | URBAN, BY COMMUNITY SIZE | | |
| | RURAL | | 2,500-
10,000 | 10,000-
100,000 | 100,000
and over |
	All	*Farm*			
1860	80.23	n.a.	5.00	6.38	8.39
1870	74.32	n.a.	6.13	8.84	10.71
1880	71.83	n.a.	6.65	9.14	12.38
1890	64.88	n.a.	7.40	12.31	15.41
1900	60.31	n.a.	8.03	12.96	18.70
1910	54.34	34.91	8.64	14.95	22.07
1920	48.77	30.14	8.85	16.44	25.95
1930	43.84	24.87	8.64	17.93	29.59
1940	43.48	23.20	8.89	18.78	28.85
1950	40.99[a]	16.63[a]	8.92	20.60	29.49

[a] Old urban definition.

n.a. = not available.

Source: *All Rural* and *Urban: Census of Population, 1940*, Bureau of the Census, Vol. II, Part 1, Table 5; *Historical Statistics of the United States, 1789-1945*, Dept. of Commerce, 1949, Series B Tables 145-159; and *Census of Population, 1950*, Vol. II, Part 1, Tables 5B and 58. *Farm: Farm Population*, Bureau of the Census, Series Census-BAE, No. 16, March 9, 1953, Table 1.

in England and Wales, whose earlier industrialization may give their experience some predictive value, an actual reversal has taken place (Chart 2.). Although our largest cities have not increased their share of the population since 1930, their satellite cities and suburbs have continued to grow—although at a decreasing rate. More than half the population lived in metropolitan areas in 1950, whereas only one-fourth lived in (differently defined) metropolitan districts in 1900.[1]

The declining rate of growth of total population is evident in Chart 1. Its necessary corollary has been the aging of the population (Table 9). In 1860, children under 15 were two-fifths of the population, and they were almost ten times as numerous as people of 60 or more years. By 1950, children of this age were only one-fourth of the population, and they were only a little more than twice as numerous as the population of 60 or more.

The decline in the relative number of children has important effects upon consumption and employment patterns that we shall

[1] See Warren S. Thompson, *The Growth of Metropolitan Districts in the United States: 1900-1940*, Bureau of the Census, 1947, and the 1950 Census.

CHART 2

Percentage of Population in Three Community Sizes, United States,
1860-1950, England and Wales, 1871-1951

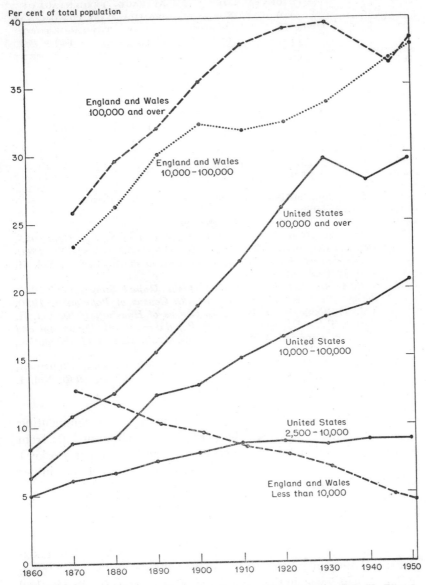

Per cent of total population

England and Wales
100,000 and over

England and Wales
10,000 – 100,000

United States
100,000 and over

United States
10,000 – 100,000

United States
2,500 – 10,000

England and Wales
Less than 10,000

Source: *Census of Population, 1950,* Bureau of the Census, Vol. II, Part 1,
Table 5B, pp. 1-7; *Census of England and Wales, 1871-1931,* London, General
Register Office, H.M.S.; and *Census of England and Wales, 1951, Preliminary
Report,* Table G.

17

TABLE 9

Population Characteristics, 1860-1950

| | PERCENTAGE OF POPULATION | | AVERAGE FAMILY SIZE[a] | PERCENTAGE OF MARRIED WOMEN IN THE LABOR FORCE |
	Under 15 (1)	*60 and over* (2)	(3)	(4)
1860	40.5	4.3	5.28	n.a.
1870	37.9	4.8	5.09	n.a.
1880	38.1	5.6	5.04	n.a.
1890	35.5	6.1	4.93	4.6
1900	34.4	6.5	4.69	5.6
1910	32.1	6.8	4.54	10.7
1920	31.8	7.5	4.34	9.0
1930	29.4	8.6	4.10	11.7
1940	25.0	10.5	3.65	16.7
1950	26.9	12.2	3.31	21.6

[a] Families include institutional groups and quasi households.

n.a. = not available.

Column	Source
1, 2	*1860-1870: Historical Statistics of the United States, 1789-1945,* Dept. of Commerce, 1949, Series B Tables 1-12 and 81-144. *1880-1950: Census of Population, 1950,* Bureau of the Census, Vol. II, Part 1, Table 39.
3	*1860-1890: Historical Statistics of the United States, 1789-1945,* Series B Tables 171-181. *1900-1930: Census of Population, 1930,* Vol. VI, Table 14, p. 10. *1940: Census of Housing, 1940,* Vol. II, Part I, Table III, and *Census of Population, 1940, Population and Housing, Families,* Table 19, p. 52. *1950: Census of Population, 1950,* Vol. II, Part 1, Table 47.
4	*1890-1940: Historical Statistics of the United States, 1789-1945,* Series D Tables 1-10. *1950: Census of Population, 1950,* Vol. I, Part 1, Tables 45 and 121.

notice later; the direct effect upon income is worth commenting upon. An economy in which the percentage of children falls from 40 to 25 will, other things (such as average income per worker) remaining constant, experience a rise of roughly 25 per cent in per capita real income.

Actually the effect upon income of the decline in the relative number of children will probably be larger, in part because of the increase in the number of married women who are able and willing to enter the labor force (Table 9). Such an increase has taken place: in 1890, only 1 married woman in 20 was in the labor force; by 1950, 1 in 5 was in the labor force. The average family size had fallen to 3.3 persons by 1950, and this of course means that a large number of families—about 25 per cent of those in which the husband was less than 44 years of age, for example—had no children under 18 years of age.

One final development in our population deserves mention: the decline of immigration. Gross immigration reached 1.2 million per year at its peak (1907 and 1914), fell sharply during World War I, recovered substantially in the early 1920's, and then fell to a low level. Net immigration amounted to one-fourth to one-third of the increase in our population from 1870 to 1920, and to more than one-sixth in the 1920's, and thereafter was unimportant (Table 10). The decline in immigration was an important cause

TABLE 10

Net Immigration and Population Growth, 1870-1950

Decade	Net Immigration[a] (1)	Increase in Population (2)	Immigration as Percentage of Population Increase (3)
1870-1880	2,530,000	10,337,334	24.5
1880-1890	4,273,000	12,791,931	33.4
1890-1900	3,239,000	13,046,861	24.8
1900-1910	5,558,000	15,977,691	34.8
1910-1920	3,467,000	13,738,354	25.2
1920-1930	3,062,133	16,611,000	18.4
1930-1940	68,693	9,045,000	.8
1940-1950	878,640	19,555,000	4.5

[a] Before 1907 no record was kept of emigration, so the earlier years have been estimated from population censuses (see William S. Rossiter, *Increase of Population in the United States, 1910-1920*, Bureau of the Census, Census Monograph I, 1922, pp. 199-204).

Column   Source

1   *1870-1920*: Rossiter, *op. cit.*, p. 204. Figures correspond to census dates. *1920-1945: Historical Statistics of the United States, 1789-1945*, Dept. of Commerce, 1949, Series B Tables 304-330 and Series V Tables 350-353. *1945-1950: Statistical Abstract of the United States*, Bureau of the Census, 1952, Tables 104 and 105. Decade estimates derived from these tables cover fiscal year periods.

2   *Historical Statistics of the United States, 1789-1945*, Series B Tables 1-12. Population as of census dates. *1920-1950: Statistical Abstract of the United States*, 1953, Table 7. Population as of fiscal years.

of the decline in the rate of growth of population. It was one source of the increasing homogeneity of American consumers.

2. The Progress of Communication

The great advances in communication since the Civil War have transformed the economy from one of widespread and loosely co-ordinated parts into a much more compact, interdependent, and homogeneous system. For we include in communication the transportation not only of men and commodities but also of ideas.

Consider passenger travel. In 1875 the fastest train required 34 hours to go from New York to Chicago, and 126 from Chicago to San Francisco. In 1950 the corresponding times were 16 hours and 49 hours, and by air the times were 3 hours and 12 hours respectively. The speed of travel by train had thus more than doubled, and by air one could go ten times as fast as in 1875.[2]

The money cost of travel rose for the trip from New York to Chicago—the coach fare was $24.75 in 1875 and $35.31 in 1950 (and air travel was $50.72). The fare from Chicago to San Francisco also rose—first class fares were $115.95 in 1875, and $123.21 in 1950 (and air travel was $130.81).[3] But if we take account of the rise of money income, the ability to travel was enormously increased. Money income per capita rose about tenfold over this period (see below), so relative to income the cost of travel (judged by these examples) fell by nine-tenths.

The cost of transporting goods probably has fallen even more than the cost of transporting people. The variety of goods and the multiplicity of movements is so great that no long-term index of freight rates has been compiled for railroads, let alone for all forms of transportation. The final outcome of the reductions in rates and of the development of new methods of transport such as trucking, however, is reflected in the geographical structure of prices. The vast reduction in the dispersion of average December prices of wheat between 1866 and 1950 is evident from the frequency histograms in Chart 3. This reduction in dispersion appears to have been general, and to have come about chiefly since 1900.[4]

[2] For the early period, see *Travellers' Official Railway Guide for the United States and Canada*, W. F. Allen, editor, General Ticket Agents' Association, July 1875.

[3] The early fares are from the *Travellers' Official Railway Guide* of 1875, as cited; the later fares include federal tax of 15 per cent.

[4] The coefficients of variation of average farm prices by states were as follows:

Year	Wheat	Potatoes
1866	20.8	36.0
1900	18.4	35.1
1950	5.5	23.6

Source: *Wheat Crops of the United States, 1866-1906*, Bull. 57, 1907,

CHART 3

The Distribution of Wheat Prices by State, 1866 and 1950
(average farm prices per bushel)

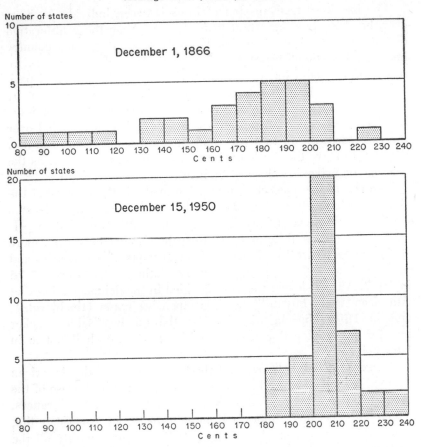

Source: *Wheat Crops of the United States, 1866-1906*, Dept. of Agriculture, Bureau of Statistics, Bull. 57, 1907, Table 1, and *Agricultural Prices*, Bureau of Agricultural Economics, Agricultural Crop Reporting Board, December 1950, p. 8.

The improvements in the transportation of men and goods were surpassed by those in the transportation of ideas. These were reflected in the postal service, and the spread of telegraphy and the telephone eliminated even the delays that once temporarily sheltered

Table I, and *Potato Crops of the United States, 1866-1906*, Bull. 62, 1908, Table I; *Yearbook of the Department of Agriculture*, 1901, pp. 713, 743; *Agricultural Prices*, December 1950, p. 8—all Dept. of Agriculture. The number of states whose wheat prices were reported was 30 in 1866, 44 in 1900, and 40 in 1950.

21

a man from other men and events. Without these developments it would have been impossible for large national organizations, economic or political, to pursue unified policies.

The improved transmission of ideas between individuals, however, has been less important in many ways than the proliferation of mass communication media. Even 100 years ago our country had an international reputation for the number of newspapers we read, and the habit has grown. In 1860 our newspapers and periodicals had a circulation of .44 copy per inhabitant per issue; by 1947 this had grown to 3.50 copies, and the frequency of issue had increased. Some 90 million radio sets had been installed over the three decades up to 1950, and 35 million television sets now threaten to make the deeds of the heroic cowboy as familiar as the troubles of Sylvania's Several Spouses.

The rise of the mass communication media is the shadow of the rise of modern advertising. Judged by advertising copy, advertising has made great strides forward in pictorial value and in persuasiveness.[5] Judged by expenditures, the rise has been even more striking (see Chart 4): the advertising receipts of newspapers and periodicals were $.78 per capita of population in 1880 and $7.76 in 1947. Advertising in the 1890's aided in the demonstration that Americans would buy millions of an expensive luxury (the bicycle), and in 1898 Uneeda Biscuits left the unadvertisable cracker box for the packaged container, with results we shall notice in later chapters.

Alfred Marshall believed that the homogeneity of the American demand for manufactured goods was a large force in the rise of the great mass production industries: "Even those race differences, which have become almost a dominant factor in American life, lessen this homogeneity but little. . . . Speaking generally all the various races in the country, widely as they differ from one another in character and aptitude, are yet alike in yielding to the dominant spirit of the strong mixed race among whom they have settled."[6] Marshall's view has eluded empirical test, and as of 1900 may have had little appeal as an explanation of the progress of standardization in this country compared with European nations. But now the homogeneity has become much greater. We have cited in this chapter some of the forces: the dwindling of immigration with the

[5] See Frank Presbrey, *The History and Development of Advertising*, Doubleday, 1929.

[6] Alfred Marshall, *Industry and Trade*, London, Macmillan, 1919, p. 147.

CHART 4

Advertising Receipts of Newspapers, Periodicals and Radio, and
Population Growth, 1867-1950

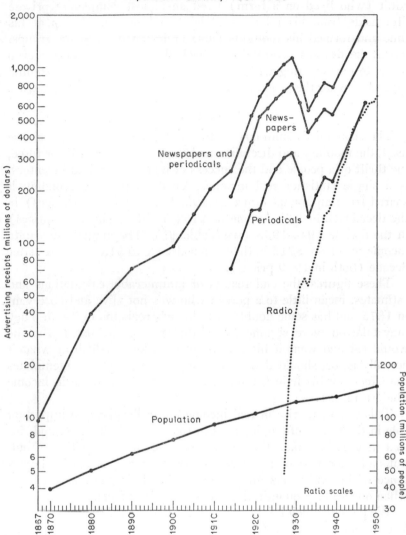

Source: *Population: 1870-1940: Historical Statistics of the United States, 1789-1945*, Dept. of Commerce, 1949. *1940-1950: Statistical Abstract of the United States*, Dept. of Commerce, 1953.

Newspapers and Periodicals: 1867: Frank Presbrey, *The History and Development of Advertising*, Doubleday, 1929. *1880-1950:* Censuses of Manufactures, Bureau of the Census.

Radio: Broadcasting Year Book, Broadcasting, 1951, pp. 11-12.

consequent decline of foreign language communities; the urbanization of the population; and most important, I think, the enormous growth of the mass communication industries. In 1860 the typical adult (who lived on a farm) lived an almost completely private life: aside from his religious activity and reading, he spent his time and formed his thoughts alone or in small, personal groups. Today he devotes several hours each day, and she devotes even more, to participating with millions of others in reading, listening to, and viewing the products of the mass communication industries.

3. *Income*

The economist's summary of the skill with which resources are used, the mobility and discipline and competence of the labor force, the thrift of a people and the success of its explorers and inventors, is a single statistic: real income. For the American economy it soared from an annual figure of $9.3 billion (in 1929 prices) in the decade 1869-1878 to one of $154.6 billion (in 1929 prices) in the decade 1944-1953 (see Table 11). The annual per capita income rose from $215 in the former decade to $1,043 in the latter decade (both in 1929 prices).

These figures, the end results of innumerable calculations and estimates, mean little to a person who was not alive and observant in 1875 and has some doubts as to his whereabouts in 2025. They may take on more significance if that person estimates what he would eat and wear if his income were today one-fifth of what it actually is, or, should this prove too gruesome, if he contemplates the effects on his living standards of a fivefold increase in income (before taxes).

This enormous rise in real income naturally plays an important role in the trends of employment in the service industries, and, for that matter, in explanations of the changes in composition of output and allocation of resources generally. Obvious as the importance of income in consumption may be, it is singularly elusive when one seeks a quantitative measure of its effects.

We possess much information on the budgets of families of widely different incomes, and we should like to employ this information to explain long-term trends of expenditures and employment. The richer community differs in its spending from the poorer community, we hope, in the same general respects in which a richer family differs from a poorer family at any one time. Should this prove to be so, we can predict that as a community's income rises,

TABLE 11

Average Annual National Income, 1869-1953

| | | IN 1929 PRICES | |
DECADE	IN CURRENT PRICES (millions)	Total (millions)	Per Capita
1869-1878	$6,489	$9,340	$215
1874-1883	8,312	13,601	278
1879-1888	9,941	17,875	326
1884-1893	10,953	21,042	344
1889-1898	11,671	24,170	357
1894-1903	14,350	29,751	401
1899-1908	19,740	37,324	458
1904-1913	26,273	44,992	502
1909-1918	36,341	50,560	517
1914-1923	55,324	57,269	546
1919-1928	72,160	69,047	612
1924-1933	70,139	73,265	607
1929-1938	61,274	72,045	572
1934-1943	87,564	96,000	734
1939-1948	153,349	131,137	951
1944-1953	230,235	154,608	1,043

Source: *National Income: 1869-1938*: Simon Kuznets, *National Product since 1869*, National Bureau of Economic Research, 1946, Tables II-16 and II-17, pp. 119-120; *1939-1953: National Income Supplement, 1951, Survey of Current Business*, Dept. of Commerce, Tables A and 1; "National Income and Product in 1953," *Survey of Current Business*, February 1954, Tables 1 and 4; *Statistical Abstract of the United States*, Bureau of the Census, 1953, Table 7; and *Current Population Reports*, Series P-25, No. 88. *Income in 1929 Prices*: National income figures in 1929 prices for the decades 1929-1938 to 1944-1953 were obtained by splicing estimates of national net product in 1939 prices for the period 1929-1938, derived from Dept. of Commerce data, to Kuznets' national income estimates in 1929 prices (Kuznets, *op. cit.*).

it will spend relatively more on medical services and recreation and relatively less on food and housing.

Several experiments were made in the use of budgetary data to explain long-run changes in consumption. These experiments were clearly failures. Because this approach is nevertheless being widely used at the present time, these experiments are reported in detail in a technical note to this chapter. The experiments do not demonstrate that income is unimportant—although income may not wield such power over relative prices as much recent economic thinking assumes—but they do indicate that budgetary information must be used in a degree of complexity that deprives this approach of most of its attractions. As a result, we shall make little use of the budgetary analyses of spending when we seek to explain employment trends in the service industries.

Technical Appendix:
Budget Data and Consumption Trends

No one will question that there are some general similarities between the variation of consumption with income as revealed by budget studies and the variation as revealed by changes in income over time. The budget studies indicate that families with larger incomes spend a larger fraction of their incomes upon medical services and a smaller fraction on food than families with smaller incomes, and generally a comparable rule holds for a nation as its income grows. Nor will many question that sometimes vast discrepancies also arise: families with larger incomes hire more servants; in modern times, as a nation's income has grown it has generally hired fewer servants. The question is whether the agreement is sufficiently close to make the budget patterns a useful basis for explaining long-run consumption trends. We present three experiments. They are reported in some detail because of the wide use of "cross-sectional" data to predict trends.

1. EMPLOYMENT IN SERVICE INDUSTRIES

Our primary interest is in the service industries, and the correspondence between these industries and the categories of consumer expenditure is not easy to summarize. In a few cases, such as domestic service, the correspondence is complete: all of the consumer expenditures go to the employees in this field. In some, like physicians' services, the correspondence is tolerably close, although some proportion of consumer expenditures go for things (like offices and equipment) which are not produced by service industries, and some physicians work for businesses. In some of the most important, however, including wholesale and retail trade and government services, the correspondence is very distant, for either the contribution of the service industries is only one part of the price (as in food retailing) or the services are paid for by taxes. We shall summarize here only those expenditure patterns that pertain fairly directly to employment in the service industries.

The classes of consumer expenditures composed chiefly of service expenditures are listed in Table 12, and the expenditure patterns of urban families in 1919, 1935-1936, and 1941 are presented in Charts 5 to 16. All the data are presented in current dollars because we have no suitable price indexes with which to

TABLE 12

Income Elasticities of Urban Families, 1919, 1935-1936, and 1941

Expenditure Category	1919	1935-1936	1941
Personal care			
Laundry sent out	1.46	1.30	1.01
Barber and beauty shops	.76	.84	.96
Health			
Physicians and oculists	.71	.82	.70
Dentists	1.53	1.24	1.12
Other medical care	1.07	.93	.72
Amusement and recreation			
Dues, social and recreational	1.29	n.a.	1.84
Movies	1.86	.97	.92
Other	2.72	1.39	1.27
Contributions and gifts			
Church	1.24	1.24	1.10
Other	1.61	1.61	1.23
Other			
Life insurance	.79	n.a.	1.24
School: tuition, books, etc.	1.59	1.63	1.64
Servants	2.15	2.26	1.82
Food outside home	n.a.	1.43	1.22
Auto repairs	n.a.	n.a.	1.13

n.a. = not available.

Source: *1919: Cost of Living in the United States*, Bureau of Labor Statistics, Bull. 357, 1924. *1935-1936: Family Expenditures in the United States*, National Resources Planning Board, 1941. *1941: Family Spending and Saving in Wartime*, Bureau of Labor Statistics, Bull. 822, 1945.

deflate the individual expenditure categories.[7] Since prices were relatively high in 1919, the curves comparable with other years should probably be shifted both to the left and downward.

The one outstanding characteristic common to all the "income curves" presented here is their positive slope—without important exception the families spent more on each category as income rose. This characteristic is measured more precisely by the average income elasticities—the percentage by which expenditures on a category would rise if each family's income rose by 1 per cent (Table 12). Most of these elasticities exceed unity, so expenditures on services rose at a faster relative rate than income. On the other hand, the elasticities were generally (9 out of 13 times) smaller in 1941 than in 1919 and the increases were on the average smaller than the decreases in numerical value. So the income elasticities for these services were high but decreasing through time.

[7] The index of consumer prices was 123.8 in 1919, 98.6 in 1935-1936, and 105.2 in 1941; average income in current dollars was $1,513 in 1919, $1,742 in 1935-1936, and $2,121 in 1941.

CHART 5

Expenditures of Urban Families on Laundry Sent Out, by Income Class,
1919, 1935-1936, 1941
(current dollars)

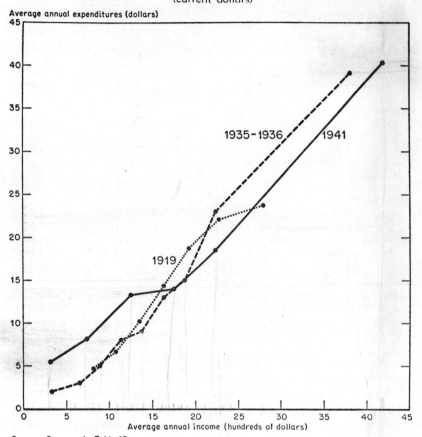

Source: Same as in Table 12.

CHART 6

Expenditures of Urban Families on Barbers and Beauty Parlors, by
Income Class, 1919, 1935-1936, 1941
(current dollars)

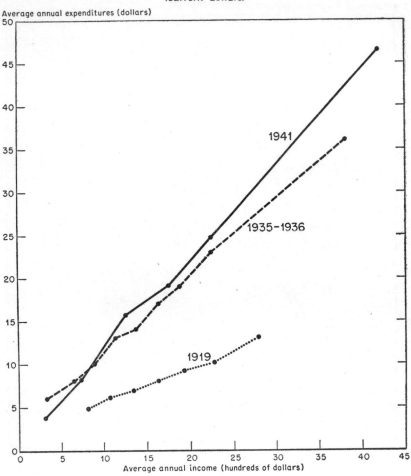

Average annual expenditures (dollars)

Average annual income (hundreds of dollars)

Source: Same as in Table 12.

29

CHART 7

Expenditures of Urban Families on Physicians and Oculists, by
Income Class, 1919, 1935-1936, 1941
(current dollars)

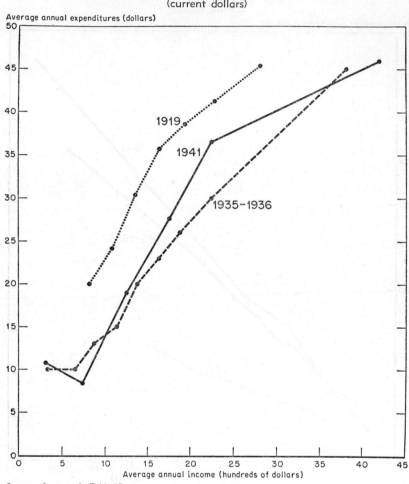

Source: Same as in Table 12.

CHART 8

Expenditures of Urban Families on Dental Care, by Income Class,
1919, 1935-1936, 1941
(current dollars)

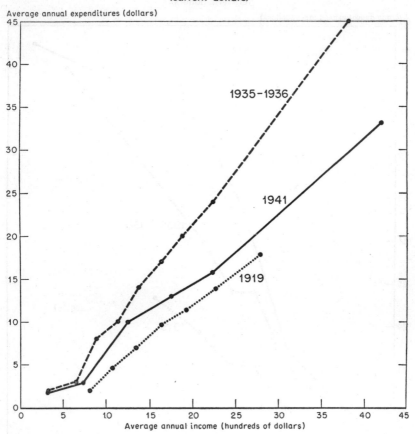

Average annual expenditures (dollars)

Average annual income (hundreds of dollars)

Source: Same as in Table 12.

31

CHART 9

Expenditures of Urban Families on Other Medical Care, by Income Class,
1919, 1935-1936, 1941
(current dollars)

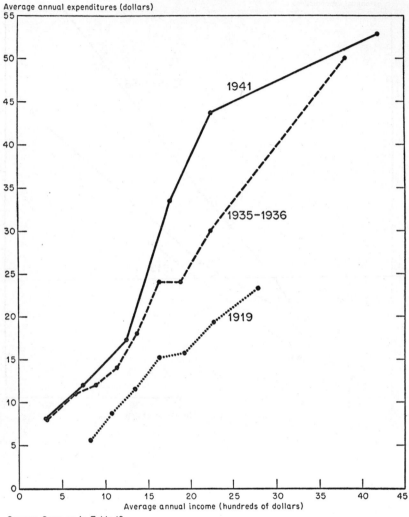

Source: Same as in Table 12.

CHART 10

Expenditures of Urban Families on Movies, by Income Class,
1919, 1935-1936, 1941
(current dollars)

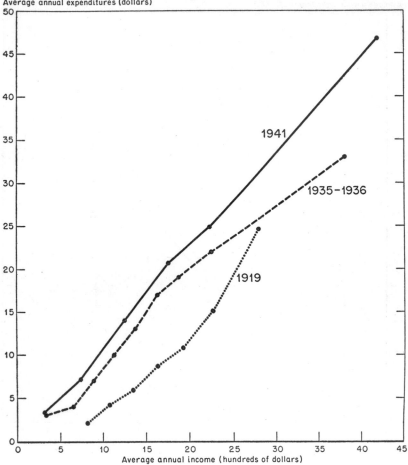

Source: Same as in Table 12.

33

CHART 11

Expenditures of Urban Families on Other Amusements, by Income Class,
1919, 1935-1936, 1941
(current dollars)

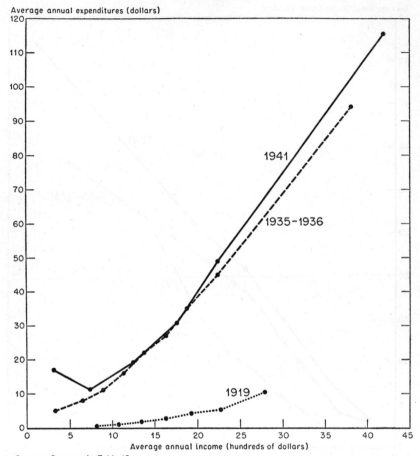

Source: Same as in Table 12.

CHART 12

Expenditures of Urban Families on Church Contributions, by Income Class,
1919, 1935-1936, 1941
(current dollars)

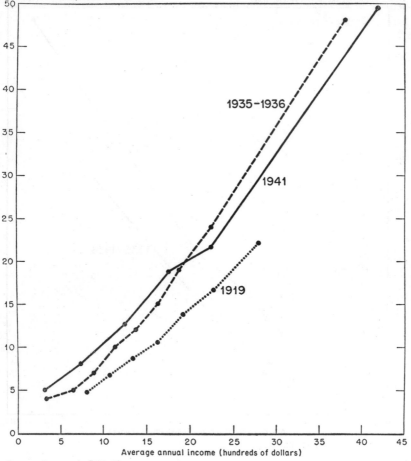

Source: Same as in Table 12.

CHART 13

Expenditures of Urban Families on Gifts Other than Church Contributions, by
Income Class, 1919, 1935-1936, 1941
(current dollars)

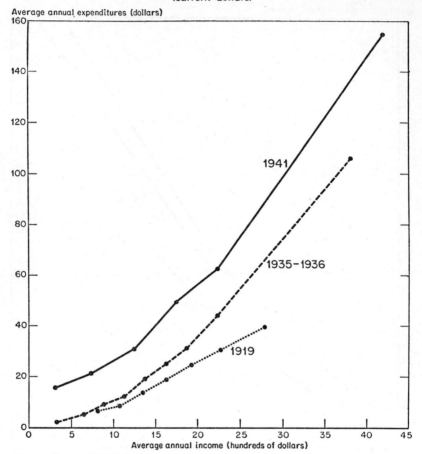

Source: Same as in Table 12.

36

CHART 14

Average Annual Expenditures by Urban Families on Life Insurance, by
Income Class, 1919, 1941
(current dollars)

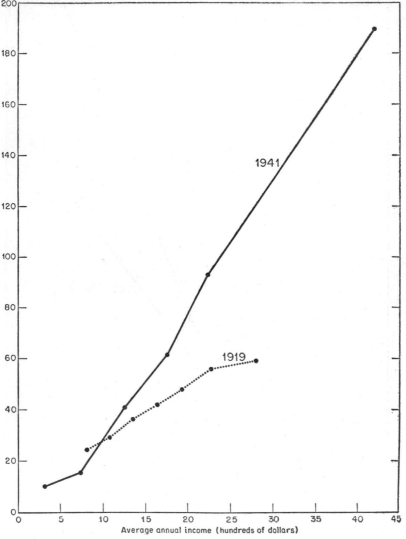

Average annual expenditures (dollars)

Average annual income (hundreds of dollars)

Source: Same as in Table 12.

CHART 15

Expenditures of Urban Families on Servants, by Income Class,
1919, 1935-1936, 1941
(current dollars)

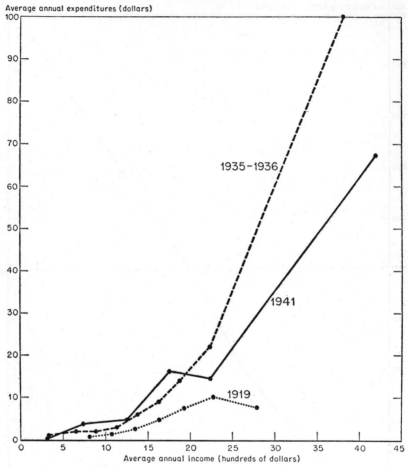

Source: Same as in Table 12.

CHART 16

Expenditures of Urban Families on Food Outside Home, by Income Class,
1935-1936, 1941

(current dollars)

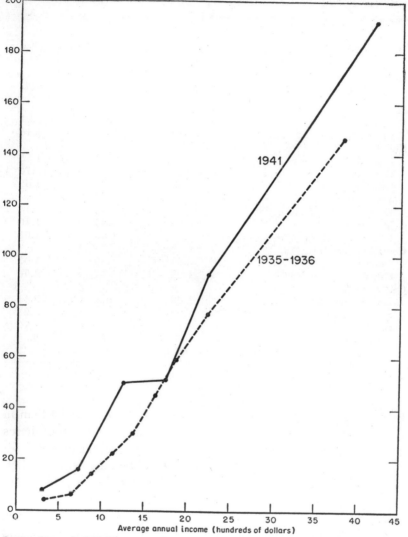

Source: Same as in Table 12.

The second general characteristic of the income curves is their upward shift. The percentage of a $1,500 income spent on each category rose in eleven and fell in only three categories (and in one of these three, physicians and oculists, the fall may simply reflect a shift to health insurance and hospital expenditures); see Table 13.

TABLE 13

Percentage of Income Spent on Services by Families with $1,500 Income, 1919, 1935-1936, and 1941

Expenditure Category	1919	1935-1936	1941
Personal			
Laundry sent out	.82	.73	.91
Barber and beauty shops	.50	1.03	1.16
Health			
Physicians and oculists	2.87	1.43	1.55
Dentists	.55	1.03	.76
Other medical care	.89	1.40	1.69
Amusement			
Dues, social and recreational	.23	n.a.	.14
Movies	.49	1.00	1.16
Other	.14	1.63	1.65
Contributions and gifts			
Church	.64	.90	1.05
Other	1.08	1.47	2.68
Other			
Life insurance	2.60	n.a.	3.41
School: tuition, books, etc.	.27	.57	.28
Servants	.25	.50	.70
Food outside home	n.a.	2.50	3.36
Auto repairs	n.a.	n.a.	.48

n.a. = not available.
Source: Same as in Table 12.

Since an income of $1,500 had a lower real value in 1919 than in the other years, the comparison slightly understates the shares spent in 1919 upon categories with high income elasticities.

From the 1941 budgetary data we should be inclined to predict, on the usual line of reasoning, the following order of rates of increase of employees as national income rose: (1) servants; (2) insurance agents; (3) dentists; (4) religious and social workers; (5) laundry operatives; (6) barbers, beauty parlor workers; and (7) physicians. (We have chosen only categories that can be approximately matched by data from the occupational censuses.) The actual order of rates of increase, from 1920 to 1940, was: 2,

6, 5, 3, 1, 4, 7.[8] Hence the income curves gave wholly useless predictions of the comparative rates of increase of these fields.

Because of the small number of categories, the rough matching
of budgetary and occupational data, the difference between expenditure and employment, and the absence of price data, this is an im-
perfect test of the use of budgetary data to predict trends over
time. We therefore turn to other areas of consumption to test the
procedure more systematically.

2. FOOD CONSUMPTION

We take twenty foods for which we know per capita consumption, and "predict" their change in consumption between 1923-
1925 and 1946-1948, given the knowledge of how consumption
varied with income in 1941, and how consumer income increased
over the period. In more detail, the steps in the prediction were as
follows:

1. Average family income in 1923-1925 and 1946-1948 was
   calculated in constant (1929) prices. In the former period
   it was $2,620, in the latter period $3,858.[9]

2. Given the 1941 pattern of consumption by income, the consumption in 1923-1925 and 1946-1948 is calculated for
   the average incomes just given, assuming that the distribution of income did not change during the period.[10]

[8] The number of persons in each group per 1,000,000 population was:

Occupation	1920	1940
Servants	14,048	15,934
Insurance agents	1,134	1,913
Clergymen, religious and social workers	1,594	1,895
Dentists	531	542
Laundry operatives	1,142	1,779
Barbers, hairdressers, and manicurists	2,045	3,343
Physicians and surgeons	1,419	1,304

[9] For the former period we use Simon Kuznets, *National Income and Its
Composition, 1919-1938*, National Bureau of Economic Research, 1941,
p. 147; households were interpolated by total population. For the latter
period we use Dept. of Commerce personal income deflated by the index
of consumer prices; households are from *Estimates of the Population of
Continental United States: 1940-1948*, Dept. of Commerce, Current Population Reports, Series P-25, No. 13, August 13, 1948, and *Households by
Type, Composition, and Housing Characteristics in 1947*, Current Population Reports, Series P-20, No. 16, May 5, 1948.

[10] The budgetary data are from *The National Food Situation*, Dept. of
Agriculture, July 1942; they are revisions of 1935-1936 data.

3. The actual per capita consumption of each food in each period, and the average retail price of each food in cities, were also calculated.[11]

A summary of these calculations is given in Table 14.

For a very few of these foods, the actual and predicted changes in consumption are fairly close (for example, beef and pork), but for other foods the divergences are often huge (for example, evaporated milk, butter, and sugar). The coefficient of correlation between actual and predicted changes in consumption is almost zero (.013). The effect of change in relative prices on consumption is more evident (the coefficient of correlation is −.328). On the whole, this experiment must also be judged a failure.

3. COMPOSITION OF TOTAL EXPENDITURES

Since the relative desires of consumers for specific commodities are less stable than their desires for broad categories, we have made a final experiment. Each of the nine broad classes of expenditures reported by the Department of Commerce was approximated from data in the 1935-1936 Consumer Purchases Study, and the budgetary aggregates for 1935-1936 were used to predict expenditures to 1948. This period is unfortunately very short, but the data do not go back of 1929, and there was a very large increase of real income between 1935-1936 and 1948. The steps in the prediction (which are summarized in Table 15) were as follows:

1. The percentage changes in consumer expenditures between 1935-1936 (averaged) and 1948 were calculated; they are given in column 1 of Table 15.[12]
2. Personal income per economic unit (deflated to 1935-1936 prices by the BLS index of consumer prices) was estimated to be $2,932 in 1948. A new income distribution with this mean, and with the same relative distribution as in 1935-1936, was constructed. With this new distribution, aggre-

---

[11] The consumption data are from *Consumption of Food in the United States, 1909-1948*, Dept. of Agriculture, Misc. Pub. 691, 1949; the price data are from the following Bureau of Labor Statistics publications: *Retail Prices, 1890-1926*, Bull. 445, 1927, *Retail Prices of Food 1946 and 1947*, Bull. 938, 1948, and *Retail Prices for Food, 1948*, Bull. 965, 1949. Where several types of a food are priced, as with beef, their prices are averaged using the weights in the index of consumer prices (*City Worker's Family Budget*, Bureau of Labor Statistics, Series R. 1909).

[12] *National Income Supplement, 1951, Survey of Current Business*, Dept. of Commerce, 1947, and *Survey of Current Business*, July 1949.

TABLE 14

Changes in Per Capita Consumption of Twenty Foods
from 1923-1925 to 1946-1948, Actual and Predicted

	Actual Per Cent Change in Per Capita Consumption, 1923-1925 to 1946-1948	Predicted Per Cent Change in Per Capita Consumption Based on Budget Data	Per Cent Change in Retail Price, 1923-1925 to 1946-1948
Meats			
Beef	9.2	11.7	118.5
Lamb	8.3	45.1	63.7
Pork	.3	5.5	89.6
Poultry	23.9	29.0	58.3
Sea food	−3.5	7.7	123.5
Eggs	18.5	5.1	37.0
Dairy products			
Milk	17.3	5.5	41.8
Cheese	51.5	10.5	60.4
Butter	−40.6	7.3	47.1
Evaporated milk	71.5	−5.8	19.8
Other fats and oils	46.7	0.0	37.1
Flour	−18.3	−10.2	68.9
Vegetables			
Potatoes	−25.1	1.3	66.2
Other fresh vegetables	28.1	7.3	27.7
Canned tomatoes	−34.8	11.9	28.0
Canned green and yellow vegetables	58.1	7.4	−4.5
Dried vegetables	20.3	−12.2	84.2
Fruits			
Fresh citrus	83.6	26.3	−7.6
Dried fruits	−28.7	10.0	21.0
Sugar	110.3	1.5	1.1

Source: Simon Kuznets, *National Income and Its Composition, 1919-1938*, National Bureau of Economic Research, 1941, p. 147; *Estimates of the Population of Continental United States: 1940-1948*, Dept. of Commerce, Current Population Reports, Series P-25, No. 13, August 13, 1948; *Households by Type, Composition, and Housing Characteristics in 1947*, Current Population Reports, Series P-20, No. 16, May 5, 1948; *The National Food Situation*, Bureau of Agricultural Economics, July 1942; *Consumption of Food in the United States, 1909-1948*, Dept. of Agriculture, Misc. Pub. 691, 1949; and the following Bureau of Labor Statistics publications: *Retail Prices, 1890-1926*, Bull. 445, 1927; *Retail Prices of Food 1946 and 1947*, Bull. 938, 1948; *Retail Prices of Food, 1948*, Bull. 965, 1949; and *City Worker's Family Budget*, Series R. 1909.

TABLE 15

Percentage Changes in Consumer Expenditures,
1935-1936 to 1948

	DEPART-MENT OF COMMERCE (1)	BUDGET STUDY PREDICTIONS			
CATEGORY		*"Real Terms"* (2)	*Current Dollars* (3)	*Relative Price* (4)	*"Final" Estimate* (5)
Food and tobacco	245.8	44.9	77.9	1.177	91.7
Clothing	222.2	92.3	160.2	1.173	187.9
Personal care	172.0	69.2	120.1	1.064	127.8
Housing	105.5	70.5	122.4	.707	86.5
Household operation	200.0	84.0	145.8	.917	133.7
Medical care	204.5	91.1	158.1	.813	128.5
Transportation	213.2	114.4	198.6	.768	152.5
Recreation	257.0	105.4	183.0	.930	170.2
Education	128.7	161.5	280.4	n.a.	n.a.
Total expenditure	201.2	73.0	126.7		

n.a. = not available.

Column   Source

1   *National Income Supplement, 1947, Survey of Current Business*, Dept. of Commerce, Table 30, and *Survey of Current Business*, July 1949, Table 28.

2   *Consumer Incomes in the United States*, 1938, Table 2, p. 6, and *Consumer Expenditures in the United States*, 1939, Table 20A, p. 84, both published by the National Resources Committee.

3, 4   *Consumer Prices in the United States, 1942-1948*, Bureau of Labor Statistics, Bull. 966, 1949, Table A, p. 44.

5   Col. 3 x col. 4.

gate expenditures were calculated for 1948, using 1935-1936 budgetary data (column 2).

3. The predicted expenditures in 1948 were increased by 73.6 per cent, which was the percentage rise of the index of consumer prices over 1935-1936 (column 3).

4. Price indexes for the various categories of expenditure were estimated, and divided by the over-all rise of 73.6 per cent to obtain relative price movements (column 4). No price index was available for education.[13]

5. Finally, columns 3 and 4 were multiplied to get the "final" estimates of 1948 expenditures.

Before we discuss the results, certain steps and omissions of steps should be explained. In effect, we assume that the relative

[13] *Consumers' Prices in the United States, 1942-48*, Bureau of Labor Statistics, Bull. 966, 1949.

prices of (e.g.) food and clothing have no effect upon the physical quantities or qualities of each purchased (step 5 above). Of course this is an extreme assumption, and can be defended only as being almost as good as any available alternative. We should expect our predicted expenditures to fall below actual expenditures for two reasons: (1) the 1935-1936 budgetary study reports about 20 per cent less expenditures than the Department of Commerce, and we have made no adjustment for this; and (2) no allowance was made for the increase in the number of consumer units during the period (chiefly because the Consumer Purchases Study "family" and "single individual" differ so from census categories). Even if we eliminated these two sources of discrepancy, the predicted expenditures would, of course, fall far short of actual 1948 expenditures because the marginal propensity to consume is much smaller when calculated from budgetary data than when calculated from time series. However, our chief interest is in the relative pattern of expenditures.

The results of this second test are somewhat better than those of the previous test. If we eliminate educational expenditures (where college attendance of veterans at government cost had large effects), the coefficient of correlation between predicted and actual expenditures was .522. This is hardly a good prediction for only a 12.5-year period. For longer-run predictions the method cannot be expected, on this evidence, to yield useful results. It is instructive, moreover, that the predicted expenditures are even less closely correlated with actual expenditures if the changes in relative prices are left out of account, so even to achieve this level of precision one must also predict relative price movements.

The lack of a close correspondence between budgetary and temporal patterns of consumption could be due to many factors, but three seem especially important.

First, the budgetary data do not portray the long-run consumption habits of consumers. In a given year many people are in different income classes from those which they habitually or on the average occupy, due to good or bad fortune, illness, etc. Moreover, when the aggregate income of the community is changing rapidly (it had risen by 16 per cent over the previous twelve months in 1935-1936), the consumers will not have made full adjustments to their current incomes.

Second, the usual budgetary data (at least in the over-all form used here) ignore the very substantial effects on spending patterns

45

(income being given) of other factors such as family composition. For example, in 1941, single individuals were 22.9 per cent of all consumer units in the $500-$1,000 income class, and 14.3 per cent of the $1,000-$1,500 class. When we add $500 to the lower income class, to predict consumption at the higher income level of the community, we assume that 14.3 per cent of the new $1,000-$1,500 class are single individuals, whereas actually 22.9 per cent will be. Since single individuals have different spending patterns,[14] this is a source of error in the predictions. It can be eliminated, or at least reduced greatly, by working with the budgets of more homogeneous consumer classes (e.g. classified by size of family, size of community, occupation, etc.) but only at an enormous increase in the labor of using the method.

Finally, over time two factors which are relatively constant in budgets can change materially: one is relative prices and the other is consumer preferences. These factors are so important in affecting the consumption of individual consumers that failure to take them into account will probably vitiate predictions. They may well be less important for the broader categories of expenditures, but this cannot be settled at present.

[14] For example, in the 1941 income class $500-$1,000:

	Single Individuals	*Families*
Food	$297	$447
Housing	207	234

CHAPTER 3

THE CLASSIFICATION AND CHARACTERISTICS OF SERVICE INDUSTRIES

THERE exists no authoritative consensus on either the boundaries or the classification of the service industries. The boundaries are not particularly important: it matters little whether government or trade is called a service industry, or, because of its size, is given an independent status, so long as it receives its proper attention.

The classification of service industries, however, is more urgent. It would be desirable to distinguish more or less homogeneous groups of industries to assist us in the study of a wide class of industries which, taken together, display great heterogeneity with respect to every significant economic characteristic. We shall therefore begin this survey of the growth of employment in various service industries with a brief statement of the (arbitrary) list of industries we include, and then a somewhat fuller analysis of classifications and characteristics.

1. The Scope of the Service Industries

The phrase "service industry" connotes economic activity which takes the salable form primarily or exclusively of a personal service rather than a material commodity—the industries which provide material commodities being designated as agriculture, manufacturing, construction, and the like. The borderlines of even this simple division are perplexing: it is not evident that a firm assembling purchased parts creates material commodities in a manner different from a restaurant preparing and serving food, although the Census calls the former establishment manufacturing and the latter trade.

As we have said, the division between the broad categories is more difficult than significant, and without further ado we list (in Table 16) the industries which we shall term the service industries. The list is commonplace in that we include none of the industries conventionally assigned to the commodity-producing categories. It is nonliteral at least to the extent that we omit transportation and other public utilities providing nonmaterial products, simply because they have been treated in earlier National Bureau studies.[1]

[1] But the characteristics of transportation and public utilities are suf-

TABLE 16

Service Industries and Their 1950 Employment

Industry		Employment (thousands)
Retail trade		8,544
Government		6,503
Education	1,539	
Armed forces	997	
Medical and health	446	
Wholesale trade		1,976
Domestic service		1,632
Insurance and real estate		1,268
Medical and health (private)		1,183
Laundries, cleaning, etc.		675
Automobile repairs		660
Other personal services[a]		321
Banking and finance		590
Welfare, religious and membership orgs.		557
Entertainment and recreation services		541
Education (private)		531
Hotels and lodging places		519
Business services		453
Legal, engineering and misc. prof. services		379
Barbers and beauty shops[b]		331
Miscellaneous repair services		286
Total		27,283

[a] Excluding the number employed in barber and beauty shops as reported in the 1948 Census.

[b] *Census of Business, 1948*, Bureau of the Census, Vol. VI, Table 1G.

Source: *Census of Population, 1950*, Vol. II, Tables 118, 130, and 133 (excluding government workers employed in each industry).

These various service industries together employed about 27.3 million persons in 1950—some 47 per cent of the employed labor force—or, if we exclude government from both totals, some 20.4 million out of a total of 50.7 million privately employed individuals. The industries are overwhelmingly those which deal with consumers rather than with business enterprises. If we again put aside government—although on any reasonable view it provides chiefly

---

ficiently peculiar so that in any event they deserve separate analysis. The studies are J. M. Gould, *Output and Productivity in the Electric and Gas Utilities, 1899-1942*, 1946, and Harold Barger, *The Transportation Industries 1889-1946*, 1951, both National Bureau of Economic Research.

consumer services—there are only five large business service categories in our list: wholesale trade, a part of legal and engineering services, banking and finance, miscellaneous business services, and a part of real estate.

2. *The Classification of Service Industries*

In manufacturing, where the analysis of industry categories has a long statistical history, groups of industries have been classified sometimes by their chief raw material (as rubber products and nonferrous metals), sometimes by their final products (automobiles, machinery). Both types of classification are fundamentally related to technology—and it is paradoxical that in the sector of the economy where technology is popularly conceived to be most rapidly changing, a fairly stable technological classification of industries is possible.

In the service industries a classification by general type of input would be uninformative—industries as diverse as legal practice and domestic service share the characteristic of requiring chiefly personal services. Since the service industries do not in general create material commodities, the type of goods produced would also be an uninformative basis for classification, and a type of service classification would lead us back to the occupational structure. So we turn to other characteristics.

TYPE OF BUYER

A first basis, already partly incorporated in the Census of Service Establishments, is the division of industries between those serving chiefly business and those chiefly ultimate consumers. Most service industries deal chiefly with consumers, as we have noted, but sizable groups do not. We can make rough estimates of the portion of sales to business enterprises in the industries where this is of importance.

At one extreme stands wholesale trade, 99 per cent of whose receipts come from business enterprises,[2] and the various business services such as advertising, engineering, accounting, and similar independent professional groups.[3] Legal service is closer to the dividing line: in 1947 about 25 per cent of the lawyers were salaried employees of business and government, and the independent

[2] *Census of Business, 1948*, Bureau of the Census, Vol. IV, p. 22.
[3] But the business services include also industries which serve ultimate consumers, e.g. window cleaning, disinfectant and exterminating services.

lawyers received 47.9 per cent of their fees from businesses.[4] Probably well over half the employees in "real estate" deal with private residential property.[5] Well over half of the employees in insurance are in those branches dealing with private individuals.[6] Aside from finance and banking, for which no estimate can be made, other large service industries deal primarily with private consumers.

There are two reasons why the industries serving chiefly business enterprises should be separately dealt with. The first reason is that invariably a considerable, and sometimes dominant, portion of the activity is carried on within nonservice business enterprises themselves. For example, the census reports a small industry engaged in duplicating, addressing, and mailing—of course the vast majority of this work is done by the business firms within their own establishments. Even a large and increasing share of wholesaling is being undertaken by manufacturers. It would be seriously misleading to measure trends in employment or output in this type of activity on the basis of the employment or output in the separately organized businesses performing a changing share of the work. The second reason for separate treatment is that to explain trends in business service industries one must usually turn to a wholly different set of explanatory factors from those found working in consumer service industries.

We shall therefore put to one side the predominantly business service industries, and discuss their growth in a separate chapter (7).

CATEGORIES OF CONSUMER EXPENDITURE

Since most service industries deal with consumers, it is natural to seek for a classification of these industries on the basis of the categories of expenditure which have been developed to analyze consumer behavior. This classification has a basic significance: The most active competition will usually be between those indus-

---

[4] *Survey of Current Business*, Dept. of Commerce, August 1949, p. 18.

[5] Office buildings, the largest commercial class in real estate, employed 87,000 people in 1935. *Census of Business, 1935, Non-profit Organizations, Office Buildings, Miscellaneous*, Table 7, p. 22.

[6] In 1939, 66 per cent of premium income was from life insurance, and 16 per cent from fire and marine insurance, and 18 per cent from casualty insurance. Private individuals are dominant in the first class, and important (through fire and automobile insurance) in the latter two. *Life Insurance Fact Book*, Institute of Life Insurance, 1953; *Spectator Casualty and Surety Insurance Year Book*, 1940; and *Spectator Fire and Marine Insurance Year Book*, 1940.

tries catering to the same class of consumer wants, so they will form a set of industries that can profitably be analyzed together. Moreover, any independent knowledge of consumer spending habits can be brought fairly directly to bear on the development of these related industries.

A classification of service industries by consumer service expenditure categories is already half recognized in the current statistics, but it is difficult to carry out in full detail. One need only mention the obvious example of department stores and the slightly less obvious examples of hotels (which derive about equal revenue from lodging and from meals and beverages) and domestic servants, whose services should be allocated among food, housing, etc.

Nor are the proper classes of consumer expenditures especially self-evident. The common budget category of household operation consists partly of laundry and soap expenditures, both perhaps better a part of clothing expenditures (which already include cleaning and pressing), telephone, which was unknown when Engel and his colleagues devised budget categories, and the versatile domestic servants. Children's toys are listed under "recreation" and adult's toys in the guise of hardware are put under "furnishings and equipment." Still, these classes of expenditure are fairly well established, and the problems are no greater than one should expect when trying to summarize the purchases of 160 million people, some of whom are eccentric.

We give a rough classification of the service industries by expenditure categories in Table 17. Industries are put in the category in which their major activity falls—thus food stores are placed under food although they received some of their revenue from other commodities such as gasoline and tires. In the cases of general merchandise stores and hotels, however, a distribution of employees was made in proportion to sales receipts. The housing category is especially rough; it includes all real estate (and hence the servicing of much commercial space) and building materials that might better be put with the construction industries.

Rough as the figures are, and important as it is to remember that we have excluded the individuals who produce the commodities that some of these industries service, the listing of workers by expenditure category is very striking. Domestic service, which was probably in first place fifty years ago, had fallen to sixth place by 1950. Education has long been unusually important in America,

TABLE 17

Employment in Service Industries by Categories
of Consumer Expenditure, 1950

| | EMPLOYMENT | |
	Number *(thousands)*	*Per Cent*
Food	4,460	25.8
Clothing	2,085	12.0
Education	2,070	12.0
Medical care	1,762	10.2
Automobile	1,713	9.9
Household operation (domestic servants)	1,632	9.4
Housing	1,164	6.7
Household furnishing	934	5.4
Entertainment and recreation	553	3.2
Community welfare and religious orgs.	400	2.3
Personal care	372	2.2
Fuel, light, and refrigeration	159	.9
Total	17,304	100.0
Unallocated		
Trade	2,038	
Insurance	760	
Miscellaneous personal services	537	
Nonprofit membership orgs.	185	
Government	2,489	
	6,009	

Note: Expenditure categories were based on the classification in *Family Spending and Saving in Wartime*, Bureau of Labor Statistics, Bull. 822, 1945.

Employment in industries in 1950 whose major activity was obviously related to one expenditure category, such as food stores, offered no difficulty. Where employment was distributed over a variety of expenditure categories, as in general merchandise and variety stores, and hotels, employees in these industries were distributed in proportion to sales receipts reported in 1948 Censuses of Business and Manufactures.

Household operations and clothing categories differ in some details from the corresponding budget categories. Household operations consist entirely of domestic servants while the laundry component has been included with cleaning and dyeing under clothing.

Source: *Census of Business, 1948*, Bureau of the Census, Vol. II, Part 2, Tables 10A, 16A, 18A, 21A, 22A, and 23A; Vol. IV, Tables 10A, 10B, 10C, and 10D; and Vol. VI, Table 10H. *Census of Manufactures, 1948*, Vol. II, Table 1, p. 401, and Table 1, p. 437. *Census of Population, 1950*, Vol. II, Part 1, Table 130.

but "medical care" (which includes social work) has risen rapidly and now exceeds personal care and recreation together—as our stern ancestors would have wished it to.

PRIVATE VS. PUBLIC ACTIVITIES

Still another basis of classification is the public or private organization of the industry, which cuts across both the preceding classifications. To the extent that private and public industries compete, as in higher education, hospitals, etc., it seems desirable that they be considered together, although preferably with full detail on their comparative roles. Such competition is substantial in only two large service industries: education, where three-quarters of the employees were public in 1950, and medical and health industries, where one-quarter were public.[7] Although we do not enter into the large subject of government economic activity, we shall discuss one purely governmental profession, the military officers, in Chapter 6.

3. Characteristics of the Service Industries

Even the enumeration of the broad categories of service industries is sufficient to indicate their variety of activities and economic characteristics. We shall now examine these industries in somewhat more detail to ascertain the areas and extents of their similarities and differences, and to provide a more useful basis for discussing employment trends in later chapters.

TYPE OF BUSINESS ORGANIZATION

The most comprehensive and detailed information on the types of business organization in various industries is contained in the federal income tax returns. The data have certain defects for our purposes, especially the incomplete coverage of individuals and partnerships.[8] Yet the obligation to make tax returns is now so nearly universal that we have confidence in at least the broader findings.

In 1945, corporate enterprises constituted about one-sixteenth of all private business enterprises, and received about two-thirds of all business receipts (see Table 18). It follows that the average re-

[7] See Table 6.

[8] In particular, when sole proprietors did not report receipts, their net profits were substituted in the tabulations. Yet according to these data, noncorporate enterprise was generally more important than the 1939 industry censuses show.

TABLE 18

Types of Business Organization and Their Shares of Receipts, 1945

| | PERCENTAGE OF BUSINESSES | | | PERCENTAGE OF RECEIPTS | | | AVERAGE RECEIPT |
INDUSTRY	Sole Prop.	Partner-ships	Corpora-tions	Sole Prop.	Partner-ships	Corpora-tions	(THOU-SANDS)
Agriculture	96.2	3.6	.2	83.5	10.8	5.7	$6.2
Construction	85.9	9.6	4.5	38.8	22.3	38.9	29.2
Mining	41.8	35.2	23.0	8.1	11.5	80.4	155.2
Manufacturing	46.4	23.4	30.2	3.3	6.7	90.0	599.8
Transportation	83.8	6.2	10.0	5.9	2.4	91.7	125.0
Trade	77.7	15.0	7.3	31.5	19.6	48.9	82.4
Service	88.2	8.5	3.3	46.2	18.5	35.3	15.9
Finance	37.6	20.1	42.3	8.7	13.4	77.9	43.3
All	84.4	9.3	6.3	20.7	12.4	66.9	56.7

Source: *Statistics of Income*, Dept. of the Treasury, Parts 1 and 2, 1945, and Dept of the Treasury Press Release S-2253, February 16, 1950.

ceipts of a corporation were about thirty times those of a noncorporate enterprise.[9] Corporations constitute a fifth or more of all enterprises in mining, manufacturing, and finance, and a tenth or more in transportation. Thus only one set of service industries (finance, real estate, and insurance) is composed to any appreciable extent of corporations; and in only two commodity-producing industries (construction and agriculture) are corporations relatively unimportant.

In terms of activity, measured by gross receipts, corporate enterprises were of course much more important: they wholly dominate manufacturing, mining, transportation, and finance, have almost half the receipts in trade and more than a third in service and construction. Corporations are conspicuously unimportant only in agriculture and the professions. Among the broad service categories, then, the only large distinctions to be found are in finance, real estate, and insurance (where the corporation is dominant), and in certain professional and personal services (including domes-

[9] If a and b are two classes of organizations, forming n_a and n_b percentages of all businesses and receiving r_a and r_b percentages of all receipts, then

$$\frac{\text{Average receipts of } a}{\text{Average receipts of } b} = \frac{r_a}{n_a} \bigg/ \frac{r_b}{n_b}$$

tic service, which is not separately reported) where corporate activity is negligible.

A corresponding analysis can be made of more narrowly defined service industries (see Table 19). We find that the corporate form is dominant (measured by receipts) in only a few large service industries: wholesale trade, department and apparel stores, hotels, business services, motion pictures, insurance agents, finance, and real estate. On the other hand we encounter also among the services almost all of the industries in which corporate enterprise is of minor importance: many varieties of retail shops, various personal services, automobile repairs, and the professions. Aside from domestic service and agriculture, these are the only areas in which the corporate form is still unimportant.

The correspondence between average receipts per business and the share of business done by corporations is close, as we would expect from the very fact that the small incomes are much more heavily taxed when they pass through a corporation than when received from a sole proprietor or partnership enterprise. A corporate enterprise with a taxable income of $10,000 in 1945, for example, paid corporate taxes of $2,100, and the remainder (if distributed as dividends) in excess of personal exemptions and deductions was taxed at a beginning rate of at least 20 per cent; an individual with an income of $10,000 paid a federal tax of only $1,810 if he had exemptions and deductions amounting to $2,500. Small enterprises are also deterred from incorporating by the legal costs of this step.

LABOR CHARACTERISTICS

Since the average establishment in most service industries is small, as measured by receipts, the employment per establishment is also small (see Table 20). There are only five industries of those for which we have data (namely, wholesale trade, department stores, advertising, motion pictures, and laundries) with more than ten persons per establishment (that is, store, shop, or separate location of business activity). The average establishment in manufacturing or mining has more than ten times as many employees as those in private service industries.

When there are less than ten persons in each establishment, and these establishments are usually separate, unincorporated businesses, it follows that entrepreneurs are likely to be a large frac-

TABLE 19

Types of Business Organization and Their Share of Receipts in
Service Industries, 1945

INDUSTRY	PERCENTAGE OF BUSINESSES			PERCENTAGE OF RECEIPTS			AVERAGE RECEIPTS (THOUSANDS)
	Sole Prop.	Partnerships	Corporations	Sole Prop.	Partnerships	Corporations	
Wholesale trade	66.5	17.1	16.4	18.7	21.6	59.7	$249.2
Retail trade	80.1	14.7	5.2	42.2	17.8	40.0	52.7
Department	74.1	18.7	7.2	15.3	10.9	73.8	162.5
Food	86.8	11.6	1.6	50.8	15.8	33.4	51.4
Liquor	76.6	15.4	8.0	63.8	20.4	15.8	62.2
Drug	76.3	15.5	8.2	51.2	18.2	30.6	62.4
Apparel	72.7	15.7	11.6	30.4	18.9	50.7	78.6
Furniture	66.3	21.7	12.0	32.3	23.8	43.9	52.3
Eating places	79.5	16.8	3.7	59.3	22.4	18.3	30.6
Motor vehicle	60.5	24.1	15.4	40.0	27.5	32.5	85.0
Filling stations	87.2	11.4	1.4	74.6	15.9	9.5	21.7
Hardware	66.5	26.5	7.0	50.5	33.3	16.2	47.1
Lumber	74.5	12.9	12.6	34.8	16.6	48.6	56.1
Personal service	87.9	8.9	3.2	44.1	17.4	38.5	13.8
Hotels	86.6	8.3	5.1	30.6	15.5	53.9	24.4
Laundries	72.7	18.5	8.8	31.0	21.4	47.6	31.9
Barber and beauty	93.2	6.8	a	86.2	13.8	a	4.3
Funeral service	78.3	21.7	a	67.5	32.5	a	20.9
Business service	79.9	8.6	11.5	23.6	14.1	62.3	32.1
Advertising	75.8	11.1	13.1	18.2	15.7	66.1	77.1
Auto repair	84.0	12.6	3.4	67.4	18.5	14.1	14.7
Amusements	70.1	17.4	12.5	18.1	16.7	65.2	51.6
Motion pictures	a	36.1	63.9	a	9.9	90.1	289.3
Professional services	94.3	5.7	a	75.4	24.6	a	10.8
Accountants	89.5	10.5	a	46.6	53.4	a	11.4
Physicians	97.6	2.4	a	91.5	8.5	a	13.8
Dentists	98.9	1.1	a	96.9	3.1	a	10.7
Legal	88.9	11.1	a	53.5	46.5	a	10.5
Engineering	88.1	11.9	a	52.2	47.8	a	13.6
Insurance agents	79.9	8.2	11.9	7.6	3.3	89.1	70.8
Finance	14.4	15.3	70.3	6.3	24.4	69.3	130.4
Real Estate	24.9	25.6	49.5	11.7	5.2	83.1	16.1

a Not reported separately.
Source: Same as in Table 18.

TABLE 20

Average Number of Workers per Establishment and Percentage of
Proprietors in the Labor Force, Various Industries, Selected Years

Industry	Year	Average Number of Workers plus Proprietors per Establishment	Proprietors as Percentage of Total Work Force
Trade	1948	5.7	16.6
Wholesale		10.7	6.2
Retail		5.0	19.7
Food		3.1	32.3
Eating and drinking		5.0	21.7
General		20.1	4.1
Apparel		6.1	14.0
Furniture		5.4	17.3
Automotive		8.3	10.9
Filling station		2.6	40.6
Hardware		4.6	22.6
Lumber		7.4	12.3
Drug		6.2	15.0
Liquor		2.5	34.9
Services	1948	4.1	24.1
Hotels, tourist camps		8.1	11.7
Personal		3.4	29.8
Laundry, cleaning		13.1	8.0
Barber and beauty shops		2.0	52.6
Funeral service		3.2	31.6
Business services		8.5	10.3
Advertising		12.9	5.7
Automobile repairs		2.7	39.9
Amusements		7.5	10.0
Motion pictures		10.5	4.3
Agriculture	1945	1.6	59.4
Mining	1939	54.3	1.4
Manufacturing	1947	60.1	1.3
Construction	1939	6.0	17.4

Source: *Census of Business, 1948*, Bureau of the Census, Vol. II, Table
1A; Vol. IV, Table 1A; and Vol. VII, Table 1A. *Census of Business, 1939*,
Vol. IV, Table 1A. *Census of Agriculture, 1945*, Vol. II, Chap. 5, Table
2. *Census of Manufacturers, 1947*, Vol. I, Chap. 2, Table 1.

tion of the labor force, and so they are in most of the service industries. They form a fifth of all workers in retail trade, almost one-
third in personal service, two-fifths in auto repairing, and probably
as much in professional services. Only in wholesale trade, hotels,
laundries, advertising, and amusements are entrepreneurs a small

part of the labor force—and all are industries in which the corporate form is relatively important.

The large ratio of self-employed entrepreneurs to the total labor force, together with the small size of the individual businesses, has been a major explanation of the relatively small role of unionization in the service industries. In 1946 the extent of unionization was estimated to be as follows:

Percentage of Workers under Union Agreements	Industry
80 to 100	Actors and musicians
60 to 80	Theatre crafts
20 to 40	Barber shops
	Building service and maintenance
	Cleaning and dyeing
	Hotels and restaurants
	Laundries
0 to 20	All other

Only two industries had crossed the boundaries of these twenty-per-cent brackets since 1938.[10]

Finally, we may give the educational training and sex composition of the labor force in the service industries (Table 21). The professions naturally stand at the top of the list of industries in terms of formal educational training—this is a basic element of their definition—but even trade, business services, amusements, real estate, and insurance have higher percentages of college-trained people than the nonservice industries. Moreover, every broad service industry employs a relatively larger share of women than the nonservice industries.

The formal education of the labor force has been rising continuously for a century, and the fraction of women in the labor force has also been rising markedly. These developments are probably related as both cause and effect with the rise of the service industries. The growth of some industries, such as the professions, was contingent upon the increasing number of highly educated people. The growth of other industries, such as retailing, was an important source of the demand for the increasing number and share of women in the labor force. Domestic service was staffed to an unusual

[10] *Extent of Collective Bargaining and Union Recognition*, 1946, Bureau of Labor Statistics, Bull. 909, 1947. In 1938, building service and maintenance and laundry employees were in the lowest class (*Monthly Labor Review*, March 1939, p. 508).

TABLE 21

Educational Training and Sex of Labor Force in Selected Industries, 1940

| | PERCENTAGE OF WORKERS WITH: | | | PERCENTAGE OF WORKERS | |
	Less than High School Education	Some High School Education	Some College Education	Male	Female
Trade					
Wholesale	35.4	46.8	17.8	84.9	15.1
Retail	39.6	48.6	11.8	70.8	29.2
Services					
Business	43.2	43.4	13.4	83.5	16.5
Domestic	67.5	29.9	2.6	11.5	88.5
Hotels and lodging	52.1	38.8	9.1	48.3	51.7
Laundries, cleaning	54.7	38.8	6.5	51.0	49.0
Miscellaneous personal	54.8	38.6	6.6	54.4	45.6
Automobile repairs	51.4	41.8	6.8	97.2	2.8
Amusements					
Theatre and motion picture	51.3	40.0	8.7	73.3	26.7
Miscellaneous amusements	41.1	43.4	15.5	84.8	15.2
Professional					
Education	12.6	18.2	69.2	34.8	65.2
Medical	18.7	43.1	38.2	41.8	58.2
Legal, engineering	7.4	33.1	59.5	72.5	27.5
Charitable, religious	25.8	31.3	42.9	64.9	35.1
Real estate	43.4	39.7	16.9	73.9	26.1
Finance and banking	19.4	54.3	26.3	69.6	30.4
Insurance	16.8	54.1	29.1	64.5	35.5
Government, n.e.c.	31.7	47.6	20.7		
Agriculture	77.9	19.3	2.8	94.2	5.8
Mining	67.4	26.8	5.8	98.8	1.2
Construction	60.9	32.3	6.8	98.3	1.7
Manufacturing	52.3	39.6	8.1	78.0	22.0
Utilities { Railroads				96.9	3.1
Communication	46.9	42.3	10.8 84.5 { 46.5 15.5 {		53.5
Electric light & power }				87.1	12.9

n.e.c. = not elsewhere classified.
Source: Summary of data from *Census of Population, 1940*, Bureau of the Census, *The Labor Force (Sample Statistics)*, *Occupational Characteristics*, Tables 3 and 19.

extent by immigrants, on the other hand, and the declining flow of immigration since World War I has contributed to the unusually slow rate of growth (and since 1940, absolute decline) in the number of servants.

CONCLUSION

The general picture of the service industries is one of small business units, organized as single proprietorships or partnerships, employing only a small number of workers in each establishment. Yet several important groups of industries depart systematically from this pattern: wholesale trade, a few selected lines of retail trade, hotels, business services, motion pictures, insurance agents, finance, and real estate.[11] The list contains all the important service industries dealing with businesses (except legal and engineering services) and confirms our decision to treat them separately from the consumer service industries.

The variety of characteristics displayed by the different service industries compels us to look more closely at individual industries rather than attempt an over-all study. And the number of service industries is such that we cannot both sample widely and penetrate deeply. These limitations will be evident in later chapters, but we emphasize here how they arise out of the nature of our vast subject.

[11] Each of these industries is relatively more localized geographically than the class of remaining service industries, excluding domestic service (which however is somewhat concentrated in the South). *Industrial Location and National Resources*, National Resources Planning Board, December 1942.

CHAPTER 4

RETAIL TRADE

THE retail shops of the United States number almost 2 million, their proprietors and employees about 9 million. Of all service industries, not excluding government, this is the largest and the most ubiquitous, and yet, as we have seen, it is still growing rapidly. The variety and complexity of our retail industry are such that no brief analysis can pretend to comprehensiveness, let alone thoroughness. We must therefore be content to survey the long-term trends in employment in all trade, then examine, so far as the data permit, the changing types and organizations of retail trade, and finally treat with some factors in the growth of trade.

1. The Growth of Trade

We know fairly little, and that none too certainly, about the growth of trade, for all its vast size. The population censuses are the only source of comprehensive information before 1929, and even they yield no industry data in 1900 or 1920. Yet the general picture of rapid growth since 1900 that can be pieced together from the population censuses commands considerable confidence (Table 22).[1] To the figures for trade must be added those in eating and drinking establishments, where only very rough estimates can be made (Table 23).[2]

The considerable difference between the industry and occupational censuses with respect to the level of employment is a reason for our meager confidence in the data. The two sources differ in numerous respects: for example, the industry censuses exclude unemployed persons, and sometimes unpaid family workers, and do include part-time workers (possibly two or more times). Barger

[1] We made estimates of trade, differing in minor details of coverage, before Carson's figures became available, and the two series agree fairly well:

	1900	1910	1920	1930	1940
Carson	2,460	3,366	4,064	6,033	6,997
Preliminary	2,191	3,435	4,179	5,905	6,756

The two estimates serve to emphasize the fact that before 1910 the figures are less reliable.

[2] These figures are rounded averages of estimates made by two procedures: (1) the average number of workers per "keeper" was estimated from 1935 and 1939 data and extrapolated backward by the number of "keepers"; and (2) the "waiters and bartenders" series was used in conjunction with the 1940 ratio of these occupations to all workers.

61

TABLE 22

The Labor Force in Trade, 1900-1950

(thousands)

| | CENSUS OF OCCUPATIONS (1) | CENSUS OF DISTRIBUTION | | |
		Total (2)	Wholesale Trade (3)	Retail Trade (4)
1900	2,460	...	...	...
1910	3,366	...	...	...
1920	4,064	...	...	...
1929	...	7,431	1,696	5,735
1930	6,033	...	...	...
1939	...	8,052	1,696	6,356
1940	6,997a	...	...	...
1948	...	11,267	2,627	8,640
1950	9,608	...	...	...

a Adjusted to 1930 base.

Column	Source
1	*1900-1940*: Daniel Carson, "Changes in the Industrial Composition of Manpower since the Civil War," *Studies in Income and Wealth, Volume Eleven*, National Bureau of Economic Research, 1949, p. 47. *1950*: Harold Barger, *Distribution's Place in the American Economy since 1869*, Princeton University Press for National Bureau of Economic Research, 1955, Table 1.
2	Barger, *op. cit.*, Table A-1.
3	*Census of Distribution, 1930*, Bureau of the Census, Vol. II, Table 1, p. 65; *Census of Business, 1939*, Vol. II, Table 1A; and *Census of Business, 1938*, Vol. IV, Table 1A, p. 1.02.
4	*Census of Distribution, 1929*, Vol. I, Table 1A, p. 47; *Census of Business, 1939*, Vol. I, Table 1A, p. 57; and *Census of Business, 1948*, Vol. IV, Table 1A, p. 1.02. Figures include Barger's adjustments of employment in distribution. All adjustments are assumed to apply to retail trade employment (see Barger, *op. cit.*, Table A-1).

has made a reconciliation of the two series which serves to harmonize tolerably well their direction of movement, although not their absolute levels.[3] Yet both types of census agree that the number in trade, already vast in 1930, grew by more than half in the next two decades.

The numbers in trade are by no means completely reported in Tables 22 and 23. We shall notice later (in Chapter 7) the con-

[3] Harold Barger, *Distribution's Place in the American Economy since 1869*, Princeton University Press for National Bureau of Economic Research, 1955. The reconciliation is somewhat forced: unpaid family workers are omitted; *all* employees of manufacturers' sales branches are assumed to be misreported in the population census; etc.

TABLE 23

The Labor Force in Eating and Drinking Places, 1900-1950

(thousands)

	Census of Occupations	Census of Retail Trade
1900	350	
1910	475	
1920	425	
1929		619
1930	675	
1935		908
1939		1,114
1940	1,215	
1948		1,709
1950	1,800	

Source: *Census of Business, 1939*, Bureau of the Census, Vol. I, Table 1A, p. 57; Alba M. Edwards, *Comparative Occupational Statistics for the United States, 1870 to 1940*, Bureau of the Census, 1943, Tables 2 and 8; and *Census of Population, 1950*, Vol. II, Table 130.

siderable number of persons who are occupied with the wholesale distribution of goods even though they are reported in other industries. In addition there are minor retailing industries which have not been included. Perhaps the largest is hotels: in 1948, about 49 per cent of the receipts of hotels were from the sale of drinks and meals, and if a corresponding percentage of the 425,000 employees and proprietors were so occupied, we should add another 210,000 to eating and drinking establishments.

In 1900, then, about 1 person in every 10 worked in wholesale or retail trade (including eating and drinking establishments); in 1950 the proportion had risen to 1 in 5. The growth in numbers was therefore large relative to the growth of the labor force. Employment in trade, and also in government, usually calls forth mingled emotions: pleasure at the jobs that are supplied; concern at possible waste in the use of resources. We shall not discuss this high problem, but we shall try to form a more detailed notion of where the rise in employment has taken place and what the main parts of the explanation for the rise are.

2. *Kinds of Business and Forms of Organization*

We shall deal at a later point with the changing composition of goods sold at retail, and the effects of this composition upon employment in trade. Here we wish to set forth only what few broad facts are available on the general structure of retail trade, and a background discussion of the far-reaching organizational changes that have taken place in this century.

Employment in the various kinds of business, or sub-industries, that constitute retailing is unknown before 1929. The most we can do is collect a few fragments from the occupational census on "keepers," that is, the number of proprietors and managers. The most important of these series are given in Chart 17. The number of keepers is a reliable source of information on employment trends only if average employment per store does not change greatly over time, and we simply have no direct information on this score. But if the change in the number of keepers is very marked, in general one would expect employment to move in the same direction even if not in the same proportion.

Grocery stores grew more rapidly than population but much less rapidly than eating places, and it is probable that there has been a substantial shift from home-prepared to restaurant-prepared meals (as the data in Table 23 also suggest). Several lines of business that increased less rapidly than population—cigars and tobacco, jewelry, dry goods—did so because their function was partly taken over by grocery, drug, and department stores. The impact of the automobile upon dealers in automobiles and accessories, on the one hand, and upon dealers in hardware, implements, and wagons, on the other, is very clear. The trends in drugs, shoes, and furniture did not differ much from that of population, while clothing, fuel and ice, and lumber all grew more rapidly than population.

Even in the two decades for which censuses are available, some interesting indications of trends may be found (Table 24). The food lines, which amount to about one-third of all retail trade, have changed little in relative importance, but there has been a rapid growth of employment in drinking places. (Since total employment in trade has been growing rapidly since 1939, however, the food stores and eating places have grown relative to population.) The trend of the earlier period toward prepared meals has continued. The clothing, dry goods, and furniture and appliance group amounts to another three-tenths of the total employment in trade, and the general merchandise (chiefly department) stores are still gaining slowly relative to the others. The stores selling durable

64

CHART 17

Dealers in Retail Trade, 1870-1940

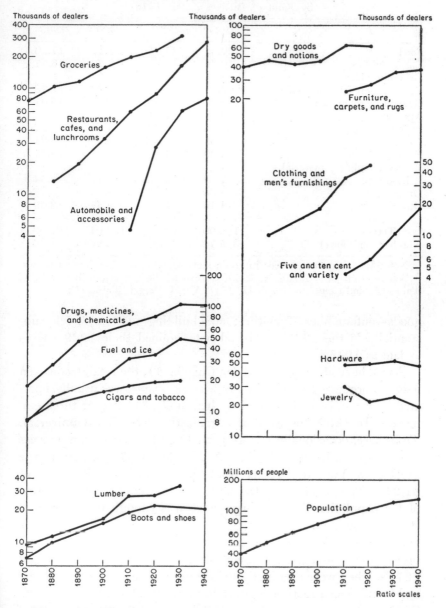

Source: Alba M. Edwards, *Comparative Occupation Statistics for the United States, 1870 to 1940*, Bureau of the Census, 1943, Table 3, p. 59, and *Census of Occupations, 1900*, Bureau of the Census, Table III.

TABLE 24

Percentage Distribution of Employment in Retail Trade
by Kind of Business, 1929-1948

	1929	1935	1939	1948
Food	20.53	23.14	21.17	17.50
Eating places	10.76	12.22	12.30	13.57
Drinking places	0	4.72	5.61	6.17
General stores (with food)	4.44	2.80	1.60	.73
General merchandise	15.08	14.26	14.54	16.07
Apparel	8.64	7.51	7.58	7.91
Furniture, appliances	5.58	3.93	4.12	5.27
Automotive	8.35	6.68	7.09	8.21
Filling stations	4.29	7.19	7.52	5.57
Lumber, building material,				
hardware	7.09	4.75	5.12	6.54
Drug	4.08	3.89	3.85	3.87
Other	11.16	8.91	9.51	8.59
Total	100.00	100.00	100.01	100.00
Number (millions)	5.72	5.34	6.21	8.66

Note: Excluding employees in chain store warehouses and central offices.
Source: *Census of Business, 1939*, Bureau of the Census, Vol. I, Part 1,
Table 1A, and *Census of Business, 1948*, Vol. I, Part 1, Table 1C.

goods—automobiles, furniture, and building materials—fell substantially in the 1930's and had not regained their 1929 shares
as late as 1948.

As we have already noticed (in Chapter 3), the retail trade even
today is organized chiefly in single-store businesses, usually operated by an individual assisted by his family and two or three employees. In 1860 this form of organization was almost universal.
To be sure, occasionally a store grew to great size; contemporaries
were properly impressed when A. T. Stewart, the owner of the
great New York dry goods store, paid a tax on an income of
$1,843,637 in 1862. But the mere fact that only a small fraction
of the population lived in large cities was enough to make large
stores uncommon.

Three new forms of organization—the chain store, the mail-
order store, and the department store—began in the 1860's and
1870's. They were eventually to take over large shares of retailing
and to influence greatly the surviving traditional single proprietors.
Their contemporary rise is no doubt partly due to the growth of
urbanization and improvements in communication we discussed in

Chapter 2. But interesting as are the problems in economic development that these new forms of organization raise, we shall restrict our discussion chiefly to their effects upon employment in trade.

CHAIN STORES

The origin of the chain store is commonly traced back to 1859, when the first store of what later became the Great Atlantic and Pacific Tea Company opened. This chain is said to have had 25 stores by 1865 and 100 by 1880, and other chains emerged during the period, but only after 1900 was growth large in absolute terms. The period of rapid growth escaped contemporary statistical measurement, but it may be illustrated by the growth of some of the great modern chains in the retailing of food and variety goods (Charts 18 and 19). (We also give comparable data on department store chains at a later point.)

The grocery chains' sales (in constant dollars) sweep upward at a breath-taking pace to 1929, and there is no general evidence of retardation in this period.[4] The rate of growth suddenly diminished after 1929 and, after a decade of relatively slow growth, again expanded after World War II. The (undeflated) sales of the leading variety store chains grew perhaps even more rapidly to 1929 and resumed their rise sooner in the 1930's. In both lines of business the sales of chains did not become large until after World War I.

When in the early 1930's the Federal Trade Commission made its extensive study of chain stores, an attempt was made to piece together the general history of their growth, chiefly from the histories of companies reporting for 1928 and 1929. Unfortunately only the number of retail stores was obtained. The estimates are explicitly incomplete, and on balance they probably overstate the rate of growth throughout the period.[5] We reproduce these estimates in Chart 20.[6] It is clear that after 1910 the growth was simply enormous; at its peak absolute rate of growth (in 1925), for example, the A&P opened 50 new stores a week for an entire year.

---

[4] We have deflated sales by the Bureau of Labor Statistics index of retail prices of food in order to emphasize the growth in volume of goods sold.

[5] All chains that failed and many (but not all) that merged with other chains were omitted, and this bias reinforces that of including the largest and most successful chains.

[6] The number of stores per chain was 4.8 in 1900, 11.2 in 1910, 23.7 in 1920, and 37.4 in 1928.

CHART 18

Growth of Combination Grocery Chains, 1913-1950; Volume of Sales
(value of sales in constant dollars, based on 1935-1939 retail food prices)

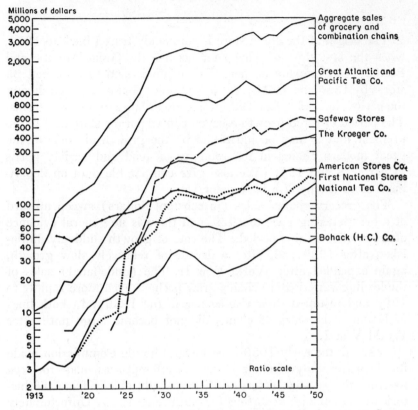

Source: Companies' annual reports; *Moody's Industrials; Surveys of Current Business*, Dept. of Commerce.

CHART 19

Growth of Variety Store Chains, 1906-1950; Volume of Sales
(value of sales in current dollars)

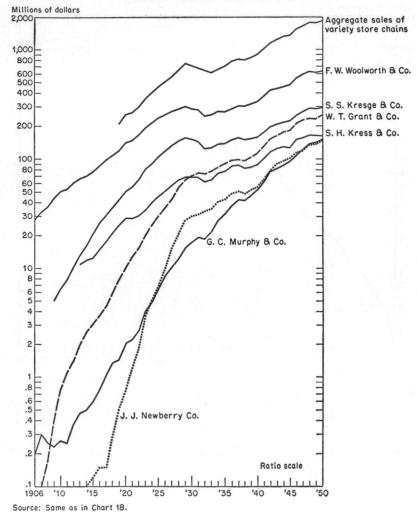

Source: Same as in Chart 18.

69

CHART 20

Growth of Chain Stores, Number of Stores, 1900-1948

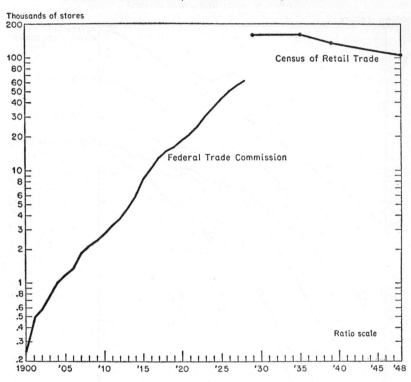

Source: *1900-1928: Growth and Development of Chain Stores*, Report of the Federal Trade Commission, S. Doc. 100, 1932, Table 35. *1929-1948: Census of Distribution, 1929*, Bureau of the Census, Vol. I, Part 1, Table 5A; *Census of Business, 1939*, Vol. I, Part 1, p. 32; and *Census of Business, 1948*, Vol. I, Part 1, Table 3A.

After 1929, the year in which the censuses of retail trade began, the relative growth of chain stores seems to have diminished abruptly (see Table 25). The decline in the number of chain retail units in the 1930's was largely due to two developments. The grocery chains shifted over to supermarkets (roughly, a grocery store with a meat market, usually with minimum service, and sales exceeding some arbitrary minimum, say $100,000 in 1939). For example, the number of stores in the A&P chain fell from 15,700 in 1927 to 5,900 in 1943. The petroleum-refining companies widely abandoned direct retailing of gasoline, partly as a result of chain store taxes, and leased their filling stations to the operators.

TABLE 25

Chain Store Organizations, 1929-1948

	1929	1935	1939	1948
Number of chains	7,046	6,072	6,969	6,159
Number of retail units	159,547	159,773	132,763	105,108
Percentage of all retail stores	10.8%	n.a.	7.5%	5.9%
Retail sales (millions)	$10,736	$8,459	$10,105	$29,737
Percentage of all retail sales	21.9%	25.8%	24.0%	22.8%
Officers and employees[a] (thousands)	1,083	1,071	1,228	1,799[b]
Percentage of all workers in retail trade	18.9%	20.1%	19.8%	20.8%[c]

[a] Excluding employees in warehouses.
[b] Including part-time employees.
[c] Excluding family workers.
n.a. = not available.
Source: *Census of Distribution, 1930*, Bureau of the Census, Vol. I, Part 1, p. 30 and Table 5A; *Census of Business, 1939*, Vol. I, Part 1, p. 32; and *Census of Business, 1948*, Vol. I, Part 1, Table 3A.

Total chain sales have also been falling relative to total retail sales since 1935, although the fall has not been rapid. This reversal of trend, following so quickly after a period of rapid growth, is attributable to various factors. Chains were subjected to increases of costs—such as chain store and social security taxes—that independent stores did not experience. One also gets the impression that the extraordinary growth of the chains during the 1920's set up counter-forces among retailers—such as cooperative wholesaling, shifting to self-service, introduction of the combination store, etc.— which have considerably diminished the chains' comparative advantages.

Even in 1939, however, the chains had substantially higher sales per employee than the independent stores in the same line of business, and much higher sales in certain lines if one takes account of the unpaid family workers in independent stores (Table 26). In the important grocery-meat line the ratio of chain to independent sales, per employee, was almost 2 to 1, in liquor stores it was almost 3 to 1, and in almost every line (lumber and building materials is the only near exception) the ratio was well above unity.

The difference in sales per employee is almost entirely due to the fact that chain retail units are larger than independent stores. For stores of equal size, sales per employee approach equality in the

71

TABLE 26

Sales per Employee in Selected Lines of Retail Trade, 1939

	CHAINS	INDEPENDENT STORES Hired Employees and Proprietors	All Workers
Combination grocery-meat	$11,855	$8,184	$6,167
Department stores	8,137	6,675	6,674
Variety stores	4,355	4,026	3,318
Women's ready to wear	7,405	6,159	5,727
Filling stations	8,118	5,839	4,749
Lumber, building materials	10,103	9,635	9,340
Eating places	3,575	2,726	2,420
Drug stores	6,745	6,090	5,461
Liquor stores	30,117	14,952	12,652
Dairy products	6,857	5,807	5,224
All trade	7,902	6,467	5,474

Note: Chain employees include central office employees but exclude warehouse employees.

Source: Computed from *Census of Business, 1939*, Bureau of the Census, Vol. I, Part 1, Tables 20, 22, 6F, and 10C.

two types of outlets.[7] This suggests that chains have had their chief effect upon employment in trade by concentrating sales into larger establishments.

If one compares sales per employee (including proprietors and unpaid family workers), the growth of chains has led to a moderate drop in employment in trade, relative to what it would have been in their absence. Sales per employee are 30 per cent less in independent stores, and chains handle one-fourth of retail sales, so at most roughly 7 per cent more employees would have been required in the absence of chains.

DEPARTMENT STORES

The department store, selling a wide variety of goods and organized on a departmental basis, emerged in this country—and

[7] For example, in stores with sales of $50,000 to $100,000 in 1939, sales per employee were:

	Chain Stores	Independent Stores
Combination grocery	$11,782	$10,518
Shoe	9,871	8,954
Women's ready to wear	7,492	6,805
Filling stations	9,938	9,447
Drug	7,305	7,369

probably also in France—in the decade after our Civil War.[8] The successful stores achieved importance before either chains or mail-order businesses in the nineteenth century. Macy's, for example, had annual sales of $5 million by 1885; the A&P did not reach this figure until the end of the century. Chains of department stores also began early: Macy acquired an interest in a second store in 1893 and Wanamaker acquired a New York store in 1897. We give the sales of some famous department stores (chains), as well as the aggregate sales since 1919, in Chart 21. Since 1935, department store sales have not increased relative to total retail sales:[9]

Year	Department Store Sales as Percentage of Total
1929	7.14
1935	8.03
1939	7.56
1948	7.24

Unlike the chain stores, the department stores have made their chief appeals through convenience and service rather than through lower prices. Therefore we do not expect, or find, large differences in sales per worker between department stores, on the one hand, and the corresponding specialty stores, on the other. In 1939, sales per employee in department stores were $7,015. In a weighted average of the corresponding specialty stores (the weights being the composition of sales of department stores), the average sales were $6,423.[10] To the extent that department stores do their own wholesaling, however, the difference is understated. But taking the difference of one-tenth at face value, one may say that the department stores by their relative growth to 1929 tended to reduce the employment in trade, but only by a slight amount.

MAIL-ORDER STORES

Although ordering and purchasing by mail has early origins, the first store to handle a general line of merchandise and sell over a large area was founded in 1872 by Aaron Montgomery Ward. His first catalogue was a single sheet; by the 1890's it had 540 pages

[8] See R. M. Hower, *History of Macy's of New York, 1858-1919*, Harvard University Press, 1943, Part II, Chap. VI.

[9] Department store sales are computed from "Revised Indexes of Department Store Sales and Stocks," *Federal Reserve Bulletin*, December 1951, pp. 1468 and 1490.

[10] See *Census of Retail Trade, 1939*, Part 1, p. 44, and Table 2-A, p. 58.

CHART 21

Department Store Sales, Relative Growth, 1890-1950

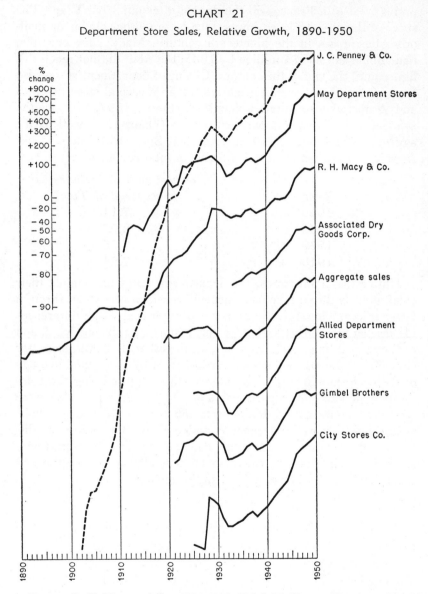

Source: *R. H. Macy and Co.: 1890-1919*: Ralph M. Hower, *History of Macy's of New York*, Harvard University Press, 1943, pp. 109, 256, 390. *1921-1950*: Annual reports of the companies, and *Moody's Industrials*.

Aggregate Sales: Computed from "Revised Indexes of Department Store Sales and Stocks," *Federal Reserve Bulletin*, December 1951, pp. 1468 and 1490.

All Others: Annual reports of companies, and *Moody's Industrials*.

and offered 24,000 items. The greatest figure in the early industry, Richard Sears, began the mail-order sale of watches in 1886,[11] and gradually expanded to a general line of merchandise during the next decade. Sears was, for the time, a prodigious advertiser: in 1898 he spent $400,000 or 13 per cent of net sales; by 1908 he was issuing more than 6 million catalogues a year. His aggressiveness and skill in writing copy were even more outstanding. (At the end of an advertisement he often added: "Sears, Roebuck and Company are thoroughly reliable—Editor.")

The rapid growth of the rural population, the introduction of rural free delivery in 1896 and parcel post in 1913, and the low prices and variety of merchandise led to an enormous growth of mail-order business in the first two decades of this century, as the data in Chart 22 testify. With continued urbanization and the wide ownership of automobiles by farmers, in the 1920's the mail-order business began to lose ground rapidly relative to chains of retail stores, and both Sears and Ward entered this area with great success.

Sales by mail order (catalogue departments) have been declining relative to total retail sales in recent years:[12]

Year	Mail-Order Sales as Percentage of Total
1929	.925
1935	1.171
1939	1.113
1948	.972

[11] Sears was a railway agent in North Redwood, Minnesota, when his merchant life began:

"Another device was shipping goods to fictitious addresses; when the stationmaster would write that the goods could not be delivered, the wholesaler would reply that, to avoid the cost of returning the goods, the agent could purchase them at 'half-price' and resell them at a considerable profit. The Chicago company in this specific instance offered Sears the watches at $12 each. . . . Sears proceeded to write to other agents along his line a description of the watches. He offered them to the agents at $14 each. . . . Within six months the trade in watches netted around five thousand dollars, and Sears abandoned railroading and moved to Minneapolis to found the R. W. Sears Watch Company in 1886." B. Emmet and J. E. Jeuck, *Catalogues and Counters*, University of Chicago Press, 1950, p. 25.

[12] Mail-order sales for 1929, 1935, and 1939 are taken from "Retail Sales of Chain Stores and Mail Order Firms," *Survey of Current Business*, Dept. of Commerce, February 1944, Table 2, p. 15; for 1948, from *Statistical Supplement, 1948, Survey of Current Business*, p. 47.

CHART 22

Mail Order Sales, Relative Growth, 1891-1950

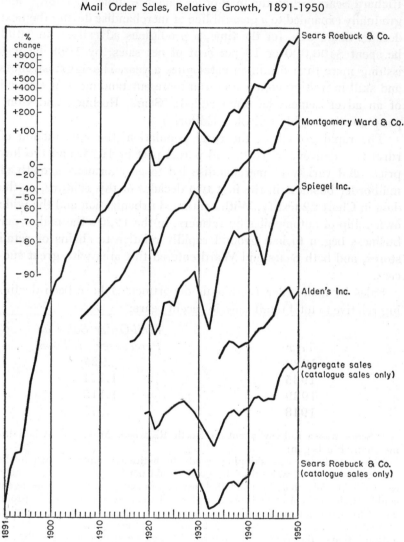

Source: *Sears Roebuck and Co.: 1891-1903*: Boris Emmet and J. E. Jeuck, *Catalogues and Counters*, University of Chicago Press, 1950. *1904-1950*: Annual reports of the company, and *Moody's Industrials*.

Montgomery Ward and Co.: 1906: W. L. Brann, *Romance of Montgomery Ward and Co.*, Champbell, Starring, 1929. *1912-1950*: Annual reports of the company, and *Moody's Industrials*.

Spiegel, Inc. and *Alden's, Inc.*: *Moody's Industrials*.

Aggregate Sales: Survey of Current Business, Dept. of Commerce.

76

The percentage of mail-order sales to all retail sales of goods of the type sold by mail order is of course appreciably higher, since many important kinds of goods (especially foods) are not sold by mail in any considerable quantities. The percentage should be at least doubled to indicate the importance of mail-order sales in dry goods, furnishings, and other lines in which these stores specialize.

Sales by mail order sharply reduce employment per dollar of sales, even allowing for the high percentage of returned goods. In 1939 the catalogue sales were $11,347 per employee.[13] In 1939 the comparable lines of retail stores (essentially department stores) had sales of about $7,015 per employee, and the figure was no doubt much lower in the smaller communities, in which mail-order houses had their largest sales.[14] It seems probable, therefore, that the rise of the mail-order houses had some slight effect in reducing employment in trade.

The first half of the present century has thus been a period of extensive change in the organization of retailing. The direct effects of the new forms of organization upon employment in trade do not appear to have been large—very probably they have reduced employment relative to sales by less than one-tenth. The indirect effects, such as the stimulation of self-service by customers even in independent stores, have probably been equally important. Even this partial sketch of organizational changes suggests that retail trade's traditional reputation for conservatism and even stagnation is not merited.

3. *Factors in the Rising Employment in Trade*

We have seen that the growth of employment in trade has been large and sustained in absolute terms, and that the trade industries have been growing relative to the labor force. The growth of trade relative to population might conceivably arise because of growing inefficiency, although the basis economists usually give for secularly diminishing returns is the exhaustion of resources and this force is

[13] Sears' sales per employee were about $10,000 in 1925, and they were also at this figure in 1915, when goods were at a lower price level, which suggests that increasing service (or shifting composition of output) was offsetting further technological advance. Emmet and Jeuck, *op. cit.*, pp. 290, 294, and 295.

[14] In a sample of 10 Iowa cities with populations of 10,000 to 25,000, average sales per employee in specialty stores corresponding to mail-order business was $5,654 in 1939. See *Census of Retail Trade, 1939*, Part 3, p. 642.

inoperative in trade. But even our modest discussion of changing forms of business organization in trade suggests that technological advance, in the sense of handling given goods with less labor, has taken place on a substantial scale. The elaborate investigation by Barger points in the same direction: he estimates that the volume of goods handled by trade increased annually by 1.1 per cent per man-hour from 1869 to 1949.[15]

It is possible that the changing composition of retail services has brought about a rise in employment in trade. For example, if consumers shifted from hay to gasoline, and the latter required more labor per consumer, employment would rise. We shall investigate this question first, and find that on balance the changing composition and nature of retail services has had only a moderate effect upon employment in trade. Thereafter we shall examine a series of demand factors, such as income and urbanization, to see how far they explain the growth of employment.

THE COMPOSITION OF RETAIL OUTPUT

From 1899 to 1929 there was a rapid increase in the importance of consumer durable goods and a corresponding decline in the importance of perishable goods (Table 27). The purchase of consumer

TABLE 27

Percentage Composition of Finished Consumer Goods, 1869-1949
(*current values*)

	Perishable	*Semidurable*	*Durable*
1869	63.2	26.4	10.4
1879	63.8	26.5	9.7
1889	64.0	25.0	11.0
1899	65.5	23.6	10.9
1909	65.4	23.1	11.5
1919	61.7	24.3	14.0
1929	57.2	23.2	19.6
1929	58.5	23.2	18.3
1939	64.7	20.4	14.9
1949	62.7	19.0	18.3

Source: *1869-1929*: William H. Shaw, *Value of Commodity Output since 1869*, National Bureau of Economic Research, 1947. *1929-1949*: Estimated from consumer expenditures, from *National Income Supplement, 1951*, *Survey of Current Business*, Dept. of Commerce, Table 30.

[15] Barger, *op. cit.*, Chap. 3.

durable goods dropped sharply during the 1930's and rose again after the war.

Durable consumer goods, of which automobiles are much the largest single component, generally require less employment per dollar of sales than nondurable goods. One may roughly estimate the sales per worker (employees and proprietors) in 1939:[16]

Type of Goods	Sales per Worker
Perishable	$5,930
Semidurable	6,587
Durable	9,522

Therefore the increased relative sales of durable goods has diminished employment in trade per dollar of goods sold. The effect has not been large, however: between 1899 and 1929, when the growth of consumer durable goods occurred, sales per employee rose only about 4 per cent on this score.[17] It is improbable that other changes in the composition of goods passing through retail stores have had any large effect on employment.

The services of retailing consist not merely of moving particular goods to the consumer, but also of ancillary services such as providing attractive store facilities, delivery, extension of credit, etc. Although no quantitative estimate can be made of changes in these services, Barger argues convincingly that they have probably increased only moderately on balance. The modern store provides less of some services than its predecessor: there is more self-service by customers, less packaging (which has moved to the factory), and perhaps less credit (which has been taken over in part by financial institutions). But on the other hand, stores have improved greatly in their appointments; they are more generous in allowing free trials and returns of goods.

These two changes, in the composition of retail goods and the extent of ancillary services, work in opposite directions. The shift toward durable goods decreased retail services relative to the value of goods handled, and improvements in retail services had the opposite effect. We must look elsewhere for the major explanation of the rising fraction of the labor force in retail trade.

[16] *Census of Retail Trade, 1939*, Part I, Table 2-A.
[17] That is, the weighted average of the sales per employee, using the weights of Table 27, was $6,477 in 1899 and $6,740 in 1929.

INCOME

The effects of changes in income upon employment in trade are not easy to disentangle from many other changes which have accompanied and been causally related to income: urbanization, the composition of output, and the like. Our reasons for not trying to disentangle the relationship through cross-sectional data have already been given (Chapter 2); here we shall explore the relationship of employment in trade to national income since 1920.

A scatter diagram displaying total employment in trade and national income in constant dollars would show a close, approximately linear relationship, and only in war and early postwar periods would employment fall appreciably below the line. Since income, employment, and a host of other variables grew through time, however, we should be attributing to income the effects also of all other factors which had changed over the three decades. We reduce, but do not eliminate, this problem by expressing employment in wholesale and retail trade (separate data for the latter begin only in 1929) as a percentage of all employment, and national income in per capita terms (Chart 23).[18] Omitting 1919 and 1941-1946 because in each period the effects of wars are apparent, we may calculate the regression equation:

$$X_1 = 15.991 + .00154X_2 + .09625X_3$$
$$(.00038) \quad (.00624)$$

where X_1 is the percentage of employment in trade, X_2 is per capita national income in 1939 prices, and X_3 is time (measured from 1931). The standard errors of the regression coefficients are given in parentheses below the coefficients; the coefficients are clearly significant.[19]

During these three decades there was a steady upward drift in the proportion of trade to all employment even when allowance is made for the rise of income. The income elasticity of the proportion, indeed, is only .06. This may be too small an estimate of the direct effect of income, but it is congruent with the belief that much of the

[18] Employment data (which include entrepreneurs) and income data are both obtained by splicing Kuznets' data for 1920-1928 to the Department of Commerce data for 1929-1938. See Simon Kuznets, *National Income and Its Composition*, NBER, 1941, and *National Income Supplement, 1951*, *Survey of Current Business*, Tables 13 and 28.

[19] The coefficients of correlation are: $R = .962$; $r_{12} = .795$; $r_{13} = .955$; $r_{12.3} = .484$; and $r_{13.2} = .904$.

CHART 23

Relation between Per Cent of Labor Force in Trade and Per Capita
Income, 1919-1950

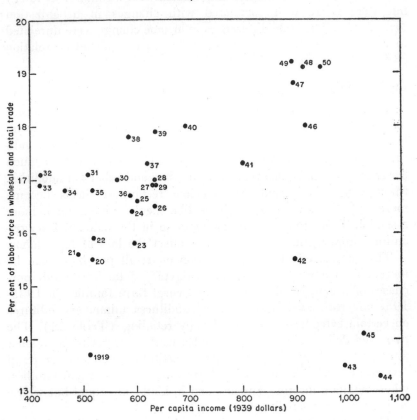

Source: Simon Kuznets, *National Income and Its Composition 1919-1938*,
National Bureau of Economic Research, 1941, Table 9, p. 153, and *National
Income Supplement, 1951, Survey of Current Business*, Dept. of Commerce, Tables
13 and 28.

effect of higher income manifests itself indirectly through increased
urbanization, changing family size, and other factors.

This expectation is confirmed by a combination of cross-sectional
and temporal analysis. A correlation analysis was made of the percentage changes from 1920 and 1940 in each state of the following
variables:[20] (1) gainfully occupied in trade, per 1,000 population;

[20] All the data except income are from the census of population; perforce
occupational data had to be used for the measurement of trade. The 1920

(2) per capita income payments; (3) per cent of population that was urban. The differences among states in the growth of employment in trade were virtually uncorrelated with income ($r = .067$) but were fairly well correlated with changes in urbanization ($r = .543$). The state differences in income change were unrelated to urbanization changes ($r = -.083$), so the partial correlation coefficients are not significantly different.

URBANIZATION

When a family moves from the farm to the city, one expects that its purchases from retail establishments will rise. The family no longer raises much of its own food so this portion of its expenditures is now made in money rather than in labor, and to a much lesser extent this is also true of wood, ice, and other commodities. Many commodities and services like restaurant meals become more accessible, and commodities like men's suits become more essential. There may also be an increase in the demand for agricultural implements and supplies to offset the loss of farm labor.

The general effect of urbanization on retail purchases can be measured in a rough way from budgetary data. The retail purchases of urban, rural nonfarm, and rural farm families in 1935-1936 are estimated from total expenditures minus expenditures on certain categories not provided by retailing (Table 28). The two chief deficiencies in the estimates work in opposite directions: purchases of farm equipment also constitute a demand for retail services; and we are comparing farm families with urban families, whose nominal incomes (money and in kind) are equal but whose real incomes are smaller.[21]

There is no noteworthy difference between expenditures at retail between urban and rural nonfarm families above the $500 income level; average incomes in the highest income class differ considerably and thus explain much of the apparent difference in this single income bracket. But farm families at most income levels buy only about two-thirds as much as urban families in the same nominal income classes. In 1900, 35.6 per cent of families

incomes are from M. Leven, *Income in the Various States*, NBER, 1925, p. 262; the latter data are from Dept. of Commerce.

[21] A given dollar income was worth perhaps one-seventh to one-fifth more on a farm than in a city in 1941. See N. Koffsky, "Farm and Urban Purchasing Power," *Studies in Income and Wealth, Volume Eleven*, NBER, 1949.

TABLE 28

Retail Expenditures per Family, by Income Class, 1935-1936

	RETAIL EXPENDITURES			PER CENT OF URBAN FAMILIES' EXPENDITURES	
	Urban Families	Rural Nonfarm Families	Farm Families	Rural Nonfarm Families	Farm Families
Under $500	$381	$280	$258	73.5	67.7
500-750	488	467	323	95.7	66.2
750-1,000	622	610	418	98.1	67.2
1,000-1,250	767	759	517	99.0	67.4
1,250-1,500	894	906	599	101.3	67.0
1,500-1,750	1,026	1,023	668	99.7	65.1
1,750-2,000	1,159	1,155	733	99.7	63.2
2,000-2,500	1,331	1,297	824	97.4	61.9
2,500-3,000	1,545	1,487	941	96.2	60.9
3,000-4,000	1,804	1,739	1,074	96.4	59.5
4,000-5,000	2,153	2,051	1,192	95.3	55.4
5,000-10,000	2,954	2,467	1,543	83.5	52.2

Source: *Family Expenditures in the United States*, National Resources Planning Board, 1941. "Retail expenditures" are total expenditures minus: all imputed income, housing, utilities, household service, laundry, automobile insurance, transportation other than automobile, admissions, personal services, and education.

lived on farms; in 1950, 14.7 per cent. We may calculate what the effect upon the expenditures at retail in 1950 would have been if 35.6 per cent of all families had still been on the farms. Expenditures would have been about 7.4 per cent less in 1950 than they actually were. This would suggest that roughly 750,000, or one-eleventh, of the increase in numbers in trade between 1900 and 1950 was due to increased urbanization. This rough estimate is too low in that it makes no allowance for the larger purchasing power of a given money income to farm families, nor does it allow for the fact that at high income levels the farm family spends less than two-thirds as much at retail as the city family of corresponding income.

We may make a somewhat more precise estimate for the most important category of retail expenditure, food. The differences among community sizes in the purchases of food are very marked (Table 29): the farm family spends less than half as much on food as the city family with equal money income, although the

TABLE 29
Food Consumed and Purchased per Family, by Income Class,
1935-1936

			CITIES		
	FARMS	VILLAGES	*Small*	*Large and Middle-Sized*	*Metro-politan*
		1. Value of Food Consumed			
$250-$500	$348	$222	$248	$271	...
500-750	401	291	308	315	$415
750-1,000	459	356	361	363	436
1,000-1,250	514	408	414	415	482
1,250-1,500	550	450	456	464	559
1,500-1,750	581	482	495	496	619
1,750-2,000	601	528	535	540	657
2,000-2,500	642	568	592	593	759
2,500-3,000	685	623	633	661	858
3,000 and over	772	728	711	851	1,163
		2. Value of Food Purchased			
250-500	147	188	227	246	...
500-750	156	252	278	293	379
750-1,000	179	319	345	350	418
1,000-1,250	200	369	397	400	468
1,250-1,500	217	409	440	450	550
1,500-1,750	233	444	479	482	610
1,750-2,000	250	482	520	528	645
2,000-2,500	270	521	573	580	749
2,500-3,000	298	562	618	643	841
3,000 and over	349	650	690	830	1,148
		3. Value of Food Purchased away from Home			
250-500	$5	$3	$1	$6	...
500-750	5	6	8	6	$19
750-1,000	6	11	12	16	24
1,000-1,250	9	17	15	24	36
1,250-1,500	10	23	22	33	55
1,500-1,750	13	33	35	48	72
1,750-2,000	19	39	50	63	90
2,000-2,500	25	56	65	84	122
2,500-3,000	30	75	98	111	153
3,000 and over	56	108	93	183	295

Note: Community sizes: villages: 0.5 to 5.2 thousand; small cities: 9.4 to 18.9 thousand; middle-sized and large cities: 30.6 to 301.8 thousand; metropolitan: 3,376 to 6,930 thousand.

Source: Various bulletins, Dept. of Agriculture, Consumer Purchases Study.

value of its food consumption is higher.[22] The difference in the patronage of eating places is even more marked. We may summarize the differences by calculating what average expenditures per family would be if the distribution of income in each of the various types of communities were the same as the distribution of income for all families, thus eliminating differences in money income. The average figures (based on 1935-1936 expenditures) are:[23]

	AVERAGE VALUE OF	
	FOOD PURCHASED	
	Consumed away	*Consumed at*
COMMUNITY TYPE	*from Home*	*Home*
Farms	$14.65	$198.92
Villages	29.17	352.93
Small cities	30.18	386.48
Large and middle-sized cities	45.20	392.38
Metropolitan cities	68.46	440.06

If we assume that these dollar figures hold also for 1939, we may readily translate these differences into employment differences.[24] In 1939, sales per worker were $6,036 in food stores and $2,427 in eating places. Hence the shift of 1,000 families from farms to (say) large and middle-sized cities would give rise to an employment of 32.0 persons in food stores and 12.6 persons in eating places.

If we choose again the year 1900 as our base, we may say that if the same percentage of families (35.6) had been on farms in 1940 there would have been 5.3 million fewer urban families than there actually were. This shift of 5.3 million families to the city "explains" employment of 170,000 in food stores and 67,000 in eating places, or one-twelfth of the total number (2.7 million) employed in these industries in 1940.

[22] The Consumer Purchases Study used prices that would have to be paid neighbors in valuing home-grown food. It was stated that these prices were higher than either farm or wholesale prices. See *Family Food Consumption and Dietary Levels*, Dept. of Agriculture, Misc. Pub. 405, pp. 364 and 391.

[23] These general patterns hold also when the comparisons are restricted to families of a given size.

[24] The differences in money expenditure appear to lead to almost proportional differences in employment in different sizes of communities. There is no large variation by community size in sales per employee in either food shops or restaurants in cities over 25,000.

The increasing urbanization of the population therefore appears to have been a large source of employment in the retailing industries, and especially in the food-retailing industries. Our earlier discussion of urbanization (Chapter 2) indicates that this source of additional employment in trade will be of decreasing importance in the future.

OTHER POPULATION CHANGES

The total effect of a change in family size is compounded of three forces: (1) the changing age and sex composition of the family, and especially of the number of children; (2) the changing income per family member; and (3) the economies and diseconomies of persons' living together rather than separately. We have already roughly taken account of the second factor by using per capita income in our analyses.

The "economies of scale" in supplying consumer goods to families of various sizes are difficult to measure: one does not know how much income to add when the family has an additional member in order to keep real income per person constant. One could approximate this figure by various scales of "equivalent adults," but we shall use the cruder procedure of holding per capita income constant because we do not have detailed data on the composition of the families whose budgets we use. A comparison of spendings of two-, three-, and four-person families on this basis is made in Table 30. Housing is the only category in which per capita expenditures fall substantially with family size, and the only categories with rising expenditures are clothing—which is hard to explain—and "other" expenditures—such as recreation, education, and reading. It does not appear that "economies" of family scale are an important influence upon consumption patterns other than in housing.

Although the large family spends more on food than the small family, holding family income constant, it consumes most of its food within the home. Every parent knows why families with young children avoid restaurants. In addition to the expense of either taking the children or leaving them at home, in the former case one must anticipate spilled water, spurned food, energetic boredom following swiftly upon delays in service, hopeless efforts to achieve quiet, and loud denunciations of the custom of tipping. The innumerable turbulent scenes have left their imprint upon the sta-

TABLE 30

Expenditures per Person of Urban Families with
per Capita Incomes of $800, 1941

	PERSONS IN FAMILY		
EXPENDITURE CLASS	*Two*	*Three*	*Four*
Food	$244	$223	$230
Housing	217	185	167
Household operations	34	28	30
Furnishings and equipment	41	53	43
Clothing	87	93	109
Transportation (inc. Auto)	76	100	95
Personal care	16	16	18
Medical care	37	40	32
Other	55	62	76

Source: *Family Spending and Saving in Wartime*, Bureau of Labor Statistics, Bull. 822, 1945, Table 20. The figures were obtained by linear interpolation.

tistics. Budget studies show lesser absolute expenditures on food consumed away from home, the larger the family.[25] Similarly, in cities where relatively many families have no young children, there is a higher ratio of restaurant workers to population.[26] Employment per dollar of receipts is almost three times as large in restaurants as in food stores, so the smaller food expenditures of the smaller family do not lead to anything like a proportional reduction in employment in trade.

The increase in the proportion of women in the labor force has

[25] The Consumer Purchases Study reported the expenditures on food consumed away from home by urban families in 1935-1936 as:

	PERSONS IN FAMILY		
INCOME OF FAMILY	2	3-6	7 or More
$750 to $1,000	$19	$11	$7
1,500 to 1,750	58	41	31
2,500 to 3,000	131	106	71

[26] In 1940 the ratios in cities over 100,000 varied as follows:

Percentage of Families with No Children under 18	Number of Cities	Employed Restaurant Workers per 100 Population
42-47	2	.63
47-52	28	.67
52-57	43	.91
57-62	10	1.17
62-67	8	1.15
67-72	1	1.98

apparently only a minor influence upon employment in trade. The chief impact—putting aside the effect that the increase in money income has on the family's spending pattern—is probably on food retailing. One would expect families with women in the labor force to purchase relatively more food in restaurants, and there is a definite trace of this effect in the data.[27]

4. Conclusion

Our survey of the factors influencing the growth of employment in trade seems to point strongly to the conclusion that certain population characteristics have been especially influential. Especially urbanization, but to a lesser degree also characteristics such as family size and the fraction of women in the labor force, have led to a rise in employment in trade relative to the labor force.[28] The growth of income seems to have been much less influential than these population characteristics in its direct effects, although of course both income and population characteristics are interrelated in many ways.

On the other side, the changing organization and activities of the retail industries have also had a substantial effect upon employment. The shifting composition of consumers' goods, and the standardization and packaging by producers, have served to decrease employment in trade per unit of goods handled. The new organizational forms, especially the chain store, have worked in the same direction. These new types of organization seem to have stopped growing relative to the traditional independent retailer, however.

Changes in consumers' "tastes," to use the economist's catchword for nonmonetary influences, seem to have been dominant in

---

[27] In 1940 the ratio of restaurant employees to population in cities over 100,000 varied as follows:

Percentage of Women 18 and over in Labor Force	Number of Cities	Employed Restaurant Workers per 100 Population
21-26	2	1.02
26-31	17	.73
31-36	39	.86
36-41	26	1.03
41-46	6	.93
46-51	2	1.29

[28] Certain other characteristics such as nativity, which we have not examined, may have worked in the same direction.

the growth of the fraction of the labor force in trade. Indeed, even the reductions in retailing services by way of persuading consumers to forgo service, delivery, credit, and the like can be considered to rest on changes in consumer attitudes. The determinants of consumer "tastes," however, are not—as is sometimes implied—necessarily subjective or capricious, and we shall find them useful also in dealing with the other consumer service industries.

CHAPTER 5

ROUTINE PERSONAL SERVICES

THE industries providing chiefly or only personal services to consumers may be divided into two classes according to the nature of their personnel. One group supplies routine services which can be performed by individuals with little or no formal training, so that many consumers perform these services for themselves. The chief industries in this class are domestic service, laundering and cleaning, and housekeeping. The other group of industries supplies highly specialized services which can be performed only by individuals with extensive formal training. The medical professions, law, and teaching are important examples.

The difference between the two groups of industries is, of course, one of degree, and it is easy to find industries whose services are hard to classify. The entertainment industries, for example, range from one extreme, where long training and uncommon talents are essential (like operatic singing), to another extreme, where only strong arches and stoicism are essential (like dancing instruction). Moreover, the boundary shifts through time: one basic effect of the accumulation of knowledge has been the shift of services from the unskilled to the skilled category. Still, the majority of employees in the personal service industries are relatively easy to classify, and since the basis of classification is relevant to important characteristics of these industries, we follow it here. The present chapter deals with the routine personal service industries.

Five of the largest industries supplying routine services are domestic service, beauty and barber shops, housing, power laundries, and cleaning and dyeing establishments; the trend of the labor force or employment in each is reported in Tables 31 and 32 (and Chart 24). There exist also a host of smaller industries providing routine services such as gardening, window washing, and the like. Some are almost fugitive in their organization, and we have little information about them.[1] The five industries we have listed contain the immense majority of all employees in the personal service industries—about 3.0 million persons in 1950. To this total one

[1] The personal service industries included in the census of business, in

TABLE 31

The Growth of the Labor Force in Selected Nonprofessional Service
Industries, 1900-1950

	Domestic Service (1)	Barbers and Hairdressers (2)	Hotels and Lodging Places (3)
1900	1,509,000	132,826	...
1910	1,867,000	195,275	674,000
1920	1,484,000	216,211	...
1930	2,025,000	374,290	682,381
1940	2,098,000	440,111	623,497
1950	1,513,000	388,805	541,959

Column   Source

1   *1900-1940*: George J. Stigler, *Domestic Servants in the United States, 1900-1940*, National Bureau of Economic Research, Occasional Paper 24, 1946, Table 1. *1950: Census of Population, 1950*, Bureau of the Census, Vol. II, Part 1, Table 124. Comparability with early years requires an incomplete coverage; the full number in 1950 was 1,730,000.

2   *1900-1940*: Alba M. Edwards, *Comparative Occupation Statistics for the United States, 1870 to 1940*, Bureau of the Census, 1943, Tables 2 and 8. *1950: Census of Population, 1950*, Vol. II, Part 1, Table 124.

3   *1910: Census of Population, 1910*, Vol. IV, Table VI. Numbers in 1910 roughly estimated by subtracting other categories, such as domestic service and eating establishments, from total of domestic and personal service. *1930: Census of Population, 1930*, Vol. V, Chapter 7, Table 2. Numbers in 1930 also estimated by deducting "eating & drinking places" from total "hotels and eating and drinking places." *1940*: Edwards, *op. cit.*, Tables 2 and 7, p. 30. Figures for 1940 adjusted to 1930 base. *1950: Census of Population, 1950*, Vol. II, Part 1, Tables 124 and 130. Figures for 1950 adjusted to 1930 base.

---

addition to beauty and barber shops, laundries, and cleaning and dyeing establishments, are less routine in their nature; in 1948 they were:

	Persons
Funeral service	59,518
Photographic studios	30,983
Pressing, alteration, etc.	91,676
Shoe repairs, etc.	67,182
Miscellaneous	33,398
Total	282,757

TABLE 32

Employment in Power Laundries and Cleaning
and Dyeing Establishments, 1899-1948

	Power Laundries	Cleaning and Dyeing Establishments
1899	...	7,448
1909	124,214	...
1914	149,100	...
1919	152,569	24,934
1925	191,072	33,666
1927	229,843	52,388
1929	264,669	75,840
1933	195,322	56,248
1935	235,896	78,302
1939	254,355	94,655
1948	316,820	230,468

Source: *Census of Manufactures*, Bureau of the Census, to 1939; *Census of Business* thereafter. Power laundries include rug-cleaning establishments except in 1933 and 1935. The number of establishments with receipts of $500 to $5,000 is estimated for 1925 through 1935 so the series covers establishments with receipts over $500 throughout.

might add the 1.8 million persons in eating and drinking establishments, which we have treated, following census practice, as retail trade.

Neither of the two largest of these industries, domestic service and housing (hotels, boarding and lodging houses), has grown in absolute numbers over the half century, and of course they have fallen substantially relative to other industries. Beauty and barber shops and power laundries have grown in relative importance, but with noticeable retardation; the recent growth of cleaning and dyeing establishments has been great and shows positive acceleration.

The common characteristic of these industries is that all supply services which in varying degree most American families also supply to themselves. The movement of work has been from households to the market in the cases of beauty parlors, laundries, and cleaning establishments; on balance it has been from the market to households in the cases of domestic service, housing, and barber shops. The movements of employment in two of these industries, domestic service and barber and beauty shops, will serve to illustrate the types of forces at work.

CHART 24

The Growth of Selected Nonprofessional Service Industries,
1899-1950

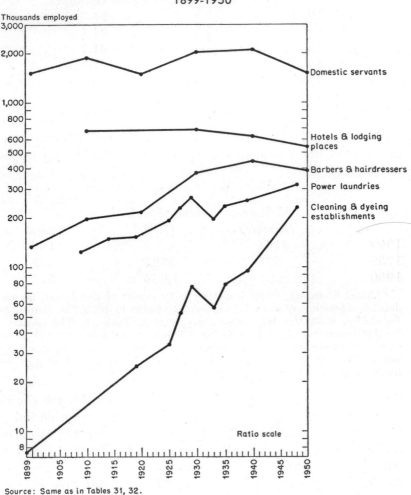

Source: Same as in Tables 31, 32.

1. Domestic Service

The largest and most ancient of the routine service industries is domestic service. It grew slowly and irregularly from 1900 to 1940, and then fell 10 per cent by 1950;[2] relative to the number

[2] Unless otherwise indicated, this section is based on the present author's *Domestic Servants in the United States, 1900-1940*, National Bureau of Economic Research, Occasional Paper 24, 1946.

93

of private families, however, the fall has been much larger:

	Servants per 1,000 Families
1900	94.3
1910	94.1
1920	61.7
1930	67.7
1940	60.2
1950[a]	34.4

[a] *1950 Census of Population*, Vol. II, Part 1, Tables 47 and 124.

Was this decline due chiefly to rising wage rates? We may summarize what little information we possess on servants' money wages as follows:

WAGE RATE, PER YEAR[a]

	33 States (Female)	United States (All)	Index
1899	$164		100
1939	375	$381	229
1950		1,036	623

[a] United States wage rate based on 1939 census of population, income data for domestic servants who worked 12 months in 1939. See *Census of Population, 1940*, Vol. III, *Labor Force*, Part 1, Table 72. The estimates for 1950 were computed by splicing 1939 wage rates to Dept. of Commerce estimates of average annual earnings per full-time employee in private households. See *National Income Supplement, 1951, Survey of Current Business*, Dept. of Commerce, Table 26.

The rise in money wages was indeed large; presumably the rise in wages including income in kind was smaller because a declining fraction of servants "live in."[3] Yet the increase was not in excess of the increase in money incomes of American families to 1939, and only slightly in excess of the increase of money incomes from 1939 to 1950; the income per family was $914, $2,000, and $4,699, respectively, in these years.[4] One may say, therefore, that the great reduction in the number of servants per family is not due to the rise in the cost of servants relative to family income.

[3] Income in kind was estimated to be $139 per full-time servant in 1939. See the *National Income Supplement, 1951, Survey of Current Business*, Dept. of Commerce, pp. 65 and 184.

[4] The figures are for disposable money income in 1939 and 1950. The earlier figure is based on Simon Kuznets, *National Product since 1869*, NBER, 1946, Tables II and 16; the later figures are based on Dept. of Commerce data.

Price is not commonly reckoned relative to the buyer's income, however, and we should also ask whether the wages of servants have risen relative to the prices of commodities and other services —in particular those commodities and services which compete with the servant. Unfortunately, this question cannot be adequately answered. The leading competitive goods and services include restaurant meals, factory-prepared food (e.g. canned foods, bakery products), laundry services, and appliances employed in routine household work. Nothing can be said about restaurant prices or laundry prices and there exists no price series on household appliances (which in any case have undergone vast improvements in quality). It is very probable that the cost of having a thing done by a servant has risen relative to the cost of having it done by a commercial industry,[5] but it would be unsafe to place major weight on this explanation for the declining use of servants. Some of the major services performed by servants are not supplied by commercial industries—house cleaning (except in apartments and hotels), bed making, baby tending, and the like. Some of the competitive industries appear to have increased their prices almost as much as servants' wages have risen.[6] Some technical developments have increased the productivity of servants, and hence reduced their real cost—for example dish- and clothes-washing machines. It is desirable, therefore, to consider other explanations for the trend of employment in domestic service.

INCOME

Servants are employed primarily by families in the upper income classes. In 1935-1936 the 2.6 per cent of families with incomes exceeding $5,000 made 46 per cent of the total expenditures on domestic service. If one estimates the income elasticity of domestic service from budgetary data, it is approximately 2, i.e. when a family's income is 1 per cent larger than another family's income, the former family spends 2 per cent more than the latter on domestic service. Yet the historical trends of servants per family and income per family move in opposite directions.

---

[5] "Value added" per unit of output, the manufacturers' gross margin, rose only 2 per cent in canned fruits and vegetables from 1899 to 1939, and only 87 per cent from 1899 to 1947.

[6] Restaurant meals may be an example. Labor productivity does not appear to be rising: salaries and wages as a percentage of restaurant sales in hotels were 30.0 per cent in 1939 and 32.9 per cent in 1950 (*Hotel Operations* . . . , Horwath and Horwath, given years).

The largest part of the explanation for these divergent trends may well lie in the changes that have taken place in the distribution of income among families. The families with the largest incomes, who are the largest employers of servants, have experienced a sharp fall in income relative to the average family since 1929, and the equalization may have been going on since the turn of the century.[7]

This hypothesis can be tested by analyzing the differences among states in the employment of servants in 1940. It is possible to estimate the percentage of the personal income of a state which the top 1 per cent of income recipients receive; the estimates are given in Table 33.[8] In a regression analysis, we employ the following variables:

X_1 = servants per 100 families, 1940
X_2 = average annual wage of a servant, 1939
X_3 = income payments per family, 1940
X_4 = percentage of income received by upper 1 per cent of income recipients, 1940

The following equation is obtained, where the numbers in parentheses are the standard errors of the regression coefficients:

$$X_1 = 5.82 - 0.109X_2 - .00024X_3 + .511X_4$$
$$\quad\quad\quad (.0032) \quad (.00059) \quad (.096)$$

The analysis suggests that the number of servants depends upon the wage rate and the share of income received by the top income classes, but not at all upon the absolute level of income. The average wage rate and the average family income are closely correlated ($r = .94$), so we cannot be certain that income is unimportant.

---

[7] See Simon Kuznets, *Shares of Upper Income Groups in Income and Savings*, NBER, 1953.

[8] These estimates were computed as follows:

1. The number of persons forming 1 per cent of the population in each state in 1940 was computed by converting the number of net income tax returns reported for each income class in *Statistics of Income for 1940* (Bureau of Internal Revenue, 1944) to population as defined by Kuznets in his *Shares of Upper Income Groups in Income and Savings*. (The conversion ratios were derived from Kuznets, *op. cit.*, Table 111.) The people in the top income classes necessary to account for 1 per cent of the population were then obtained.

2. The aggregate income of the upper 1 per cent of the population was computed by converting the net income, tax definition, for the income classes found in step 1 to economic income, as defined by Kuznets. (Conversion ratios derived from Kuznets, *op. cit.*, Table 112.)

3. The total economic income received by the upper 1 per cent of the population was then compared with state income payments.

TABLE 33

Percentage of Income Payments Received
by Upper 1 Per Cent of Recipients, 1940

	Percentage		*Percentage*
Alabama	11.86	Montana	7.25
Arizona	8.38	Nebraska	9.30
Arkansas	10.87	Nevada	12.61
California	9.00	New Hampshire	10.10
Colorado	10.12	New Jersey	11.16
Connecticut	13.45	New Mexico	10.04
Delaware	31.99	New York	11.78
District of Columbia	7.57	North Carolina	11.29
Florida	16.13	North Dakota	6.18
Georgia	13.33	Ohio	10.95
Idaho	6.37	Oklahoma	10.50
Illinois	11.08	Pennsylvania	11.25
Indiana	9.53	Oregon	8.93
Iowa	9.60	Rhode Island	11.94
Kansas	8.28	South Carolina	9.50
Kentucky	11.22	South Dakota	6.36
Louisiana	11.69	Tennessee	13.01
Maine	10.03	Texas	11.58
Maryland	12.24	Utah	8.37
Massachusetts	10.80	Vermont	9.07
Michigan	11.33	Virginia	11.91
Minnesota	9.57	Washington	7.67
Mississippi	11.92	West Virginia	9.45
Missouri	11.66	Wisconsin	9.41
		Wyoming	8.46

Source: *Statistics of Income for 1940*, Bureau of Internal Revenue, Part 1, 1944, Table 8; Simon Kuznets, *Shares of Upper Income Groups in Income and Savings*, National Bureau of Economic Research, 1953; and *Survey of Current Business*, Dept. of Commerce, August 1952, p. 16.

But it is noteworthy that in international comparisons one finds that some of the poorest countries make the largest use of servants.[0]

POPULATION CHARACTERISTICS

At higher income levels, the urban family spends much more than the farm family for domestic service (Table 34). If we weight

[9] The following data unfortunately cannot be supplemented by income

the expenditures of the four income classes of Table 34 by the total number of families in each class, we may summarize the table as follows: if all families had been on farms, average family expenditures on servants would have been $11; if all families had

TABLE 34

Family Expenditures for Household Service, by Income Class,
1935-1936

	Urban Families	Rural Nonfarm Families	Farm Families
$500 to $1,000	$2	$4	$3
1,500 to 2,000	11	27	12
3,000 to 4,000	80	95	31
5,000 to 10,000	278	154	87

Source: *Family Expenditures in the United States*, National Resources Planning Board, 1941, Table 30.

been in cities, $21. But wages of servants are much lower in rural than in urban areas, so the expenditure data greatly exaggerate the influence of urbanization on employment of servants. Fragmentary data on employment suggest that nonfarm families employ

distribution data, but the high ratios in India, South Africa, and England in 1931 support the view that the income distribution is influential:

Country	Year	Servants per 1,000 Population
United States	1940	15.9
England	1931	37.1
	1951	17.4
Germany	1933	19.5
Canada	1941	13.6
India	1931	35.9
South Africa	1936	43.7

Country	Source
India	Statistical Abstract for British India, 1930-1933 to 1939-1940.
South Africa	Sixth Census of the Union of South Africa, Population, Vol. I, Occupations and Industry, Vol. VII.
Canada	Eighth Census of Canada, Vols. I and VII.
England	General Register Office, 1951, One Per cent Sample, Table, Part I.
Other	George J. Stigler, *Domestic Servants in the United States, 1900-1940*, National Bureau of Economic Research, Occasional Paper 24, 1946.

more domestic servants than farm families, but that the number of servants per family does not increase with city size.[10]

The declining number of children per family, on the other hand, has worked in the direction of decreasing the demand for servants. Budgetary data suggest that expenditures on servants are larger, the larger the number of children, but that the increase of expenditures with family size is smaller as family income becomes larger.

[10] The following data, which point in this direction, are from the Consumer Purchases Study:

	FAMILY INCOME			
	$2,500-$3,000		*$5,000-$7,500*	
AREA	*Expenditure on Servants*	*Average Weeks of Servant Services*	*Expenditure on Servants*	*Average Weeks of Servant Services*
New York[a]	$21.90	6.9	$368.80	50.1
Chicago[a]	28.40	8.9	245.10	45.7
Columbus, Ohio[a]	28.10	10.3	249.60	51.2
Providence[a]	32.60	10.8	233.60	46.8
East Central middle-sized cities[a]	33.50	10.5	235.20[b]	50.4[b]
West Central middle-sized cities[a]	52.50	18.1	223.60[b]	48.6[b]
East Central small cities[c]	30.40	10.5		
North Central small cities[c]	36.12	9.7	179.84[d]	41.3[d,e]
Middle Atlantic and North Central villages[f]	27.14	6.7	121.70[d]	33 [d,e]
Penn.-Ohio farms[f]	18.61	6.2	22.11[d]	7.8[d,e]
California farms[f]	29.87	4.4	137.10	22.6[d,e]

[a] Taken from *Family Expenditures in Selected Cities, 1935-36*, Bureau of Labor Statistics, Vol. I, *Housing*, Bull. 648, 1941, Table 8.

[b] Income of $5,000 or more.

[c] Hazel Kyrk, *et al.*, *Family Expenditures for Housing and Household Operation*, Dept. of Agriculture, *Urban and Village Series*, Misc. Pub. 432, 1941, Table 48.

[d] Income of $5,000 to $10,000.

[e] Estimated as one-sixth of number of days.

[f] Hazel Kyrk, *et al.*, *Family Expenditures for Housing and Household Operation*, *Five Regions*, Dept. of Agriculture, *Farm Series*, Misc. Pub. 457, 1941, Table 40.

TECHNOLOGY

During the first half of the twentieth century, large changes occurred in the households of the country. In 1900 most houses were heated with coal or wood; in 1950 one-third were heated by gas or petroleum products. In 1900 most homes cooked with coal or wood; in 1950 three-fourths had shifted to gas or electricity. In 1900 there were only ineffective hand washing machines, no dish-washing machines, no electric toasters, no vacuum cleaners, and only primitive ironing equipment.

Much of the task of preparing food for consumption within the home—to say nothing of the increased patronage of restaurants— has been taken over by commercial industry. Bakeries now make the bread, and canneries preserve the fruits and vegetables, that were once the task of the housewife or her servants. An ever-growing list of foods are now fully prepared, except for the heating, for household consumption.

Not all of these technological advances reduce the demand for servants—the washing machine, for example, has probably shifted much laundering from hand and power laundries to the household, where it gives rise to a demand for domestic service. On balance, however, these advances have reduced greatly the irksomeness and time required by the performance of household chores, and together with the decreasing inequality of income distribution probably explain a major part of the decline of domestic service relative to the population.

THE SUPPLY OF SERVANTS

In 1930, almost half of the female servants were Negroes, and even though immigration had almost halted, one-seventh of the servants were still foreign-born white women. Domestic service was also the major employment for both classes of women: 54 per cent of Negro working women and 27 per cent of foreign-born white working women were in domestic service. The importance of Negro and immigrant workers in domestic service has probably been due to both the absence of educational qualifications for domestic service and the practice of discrimination against these groups in many other industries.

New additions to the supply of immigrant servants have almost vanished. The employment of Negro women in other industries has increased greatly.[11] But the competition of other industries for Negro women has not yet become a strong force in reducing the number of servants: between 1940 and 1950 the full-time earnings of a servant rose from $533 to $1,414, or by 165 per cent, whereas the full-time earnings of all workers rose from $1,306 to $3,024, or by 132 per cent.[12]

2. *Barber and Beauty Shops*

The workers in barber and beauty shops have not been separated in the population censuses, but if we identify them by sex, the two branches of the industry have had very different histories (Table 35).[13] The number of barbers has not grown as rapidly as the male

TABLE 35
Barbers, Hairdressers, etc., 1900-1950

	TOTAL NUMBER		MALE WORKERS PER 1,000 MALES IN POPULATION	FEMALE WORKERS PER 1,000 FEMALES IN POPULATION
	Male	*Female*		
1900	125,542	7,284	3.23	.20
1910	172,977	22,298	3.65	.50
1920	182,965	33,246	3.39	.64
1930	261,096	113,194	4.20	1.87
1940	221,979	218,132	3.36	3.32
1950	195,369	193,436	2.61	2.55

Source: Alba M. Edwards, *Comparative Occupation Statistics for the United States, 1870 to 1940*, Bureau of the Census, 1943, Tables 2, 9, and 10, and *Census of Population, 1950*, Bureau of the Census, Vol. II, Part 1, Table 124.

population, while the number of workers in beauty parlors has increased many fold more than the female population. It would be gratuitous to associate this divergence of trend with the increasing ratio of female to male population.

[11] In 1940 there were 1.5 million employed Negro women in the labor force, of whom 60.3 per cent were in domestic service and 16.0 per cent in agriculture. In 1950 there were 1.9 million Negro women in the labor force, of whom 42.1 per cent were in domestic service and 9.2 per cent in agriculture.

[12] *National Income Supplement, 1951, Survey of Current Business*, Table 26.

[13] In 1939, women were 3.8 per cent of the employees of barber shops and 91.9 per cent of the employees of beauty parlors.

The proximate explanation of the slower growth (and absolute decline) of the barber trade is that men now shave themselves. Early in the century, King C. Gillette began the commercial development of the safety razor, and his company's sales rose from 91,000 razors in the first full year (1904) to 451,000 in 1915. Thereafter the popularity of the safety razor was much increased when the government gave a razor to each soldier in World War I. Wider use was also encouraged by the fall in price: for a decade or more the price of a razor, with twelve blades, was $5, and it was still $3.65 in 1920, but the price fell to $1 in 1921 when Gillette's patent expired. In the 1930's the electric shaver appeared, and by 1947 its annual sales had grown to 2.5 million. The decline in the number of barbers relative to the number of males in urban centers (they are the chief customers) came only after 1910, but by 1950 the ratio had fallen two-fifths from its peak.[14]

Conversely, the rapid growth of the beauty parlor industry was fostered for a time by technology. Charles Nessler invented the basic machine for "permanent" waving in 1905; for a time growth was slow,[15] but it was estimated that by 1925 more than 2 million permanent waves were given annually. In the 1930's, cold waving was developed, and in the 1940's the rapid expansion of home waving kits led to a large scale return of hair waving to the household.

Changing tastes in personal appearance, however, have probably been more important than changes in technology. The era of bobbed hair, which reached a climax in 1928 when Mary Pickford cut her hair, led to a vast expansion of the beauty parlors. The increasing number of women in the labor force probably patronized the beauty parlors more than they would have as housewives.[16] When the American male decided to be close- and more or less continuously shaven, it was not likely that he would spend 15 or 30 minutes a day in a barber shop.

[14] The pattern was similar for the urban population alone.

[15] "In 1909," Mr. Nessler states, "only 72 women in the entire world boasted of a permanent wave," and presumably all who had them boasted. H. J. Smith, "The Growth of the Beauty Profession," *Hair and Beauty Science*, June 1928.

[16] In 1939, in 92 cities with population exceeding 100,000, the coefficient of correlation between beauty parlor receipts per family and percentage of families with no children under 18 was .618. This correlation probably reflects the greater tendency of wives without young children to work and hence the greater availability of income.

One expects that expenditures on personal care will be fairly responsive to consumer incomes, and the data confirm the expectation. The budgetary data (Table 36) suggest that expenditures on personal care increase relatively almost as fast as income in the lower and middle income classes (the income elasticity is about

TABLE 36

Family Expenditures for Personal Care, by Income Class,
1935-1936

	Urban Families	Rural Nonfarm Families	Farm Families
$500 to $1,000	$19	$18	$11
1,500 to 2,000	37	36	23
3,000 to 4,000	63	56	35
5,000 to 10,000	98	89	48

Source: *Family Expenditures in the United States*, National Resources Planning Board, 1941, Table 38.

+1 in each type of community) but increase at a relatively slower rate in the upper income classes. The temporal data on consumer expenditures (Chart 25) suggest a similar conclusion for barbers: expenditures increase in slower proportion than disposable income. The expenditures on beauty parlors, however, indicate that there has been a radical change in the relationship to income since 1946, which, if correctly reported, is presumably attributable to the development of home waving kits.

Both the barber and beauty parlor industries are organized in small shops, operated chiefly by single proprietors.[17] In 1948, only 16 barber shops and 159 beauty parlors reported receipts of $100,-000 or more, and average receipts per establishment were $4,400 and $5,400 respectively.

Almost all states have passed licensing, and a few states also price-fixing, statutes, at the petition of the barbering and beauty parlor trades.[18] These statutes commonly prescribe a minimum ap-

[17] Only 200 of 84,083 barber shops, and 1,360 of 65,694 beauty parlors, were owned by corporations in 1948.

[18] See "Working Conditions and Wages in Union Barber Shops, 1938," *Monthly Labor Review*, June 1939; David Fellman, "A Case Study in Administrative Law—The Regulation of Barbers," *Washington University Law Quarterly*, February 1941, pp. 213-242; and W. F. Brown and R. Cassady, "Guild Pricing in the Service Trades," *Quarterly Journal of Economics*, February 1947, pp. 311-338.

CHART 25

Personal Consumption Expenditures on Barber Shop and Beauty Parlor
Services, and Disposable Personal Income, 1929-1950

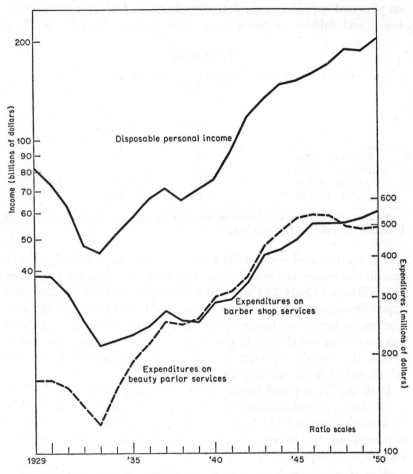

Source: *National Income Supplement, 1951, Survey of Current Business*, Dept. of Commerce.

prenticeship averaging eighteen months, but sometimes for so extraordinary a period as three years, and state examination by boards consisting of barbers and cosmeticians. In Table 37, the number of barbers relative to population, and salaries of full-time barbers, are compared for states with different periods of apprenticeship.[19] If the apprenticeship requirements were effective, one

[19] The apprenticeship periods are as of 1939. Since many of the laws governing barbers were passed in the 1930's, it was believed that 1948 employment and wage data would better reflect their full effects.

104

TABLE 37

Number and Earnings (Full-Time) of Barbers in Selected
States, 1948, by Apprenticeship Period

STATES AND PER CAPITA INCOME	PERIOD OF REQUIRED APPRENTICESHIP (MONTHS)				
	6	*12*	*18*	*24*	*36*
Number of states	2	7	22	6	3
Average per capita income	$1,379	$1,019	$1,303	$1,459	$1,563
	Barbers per 10,000 Male Population				
All states	20.62	17.42	19.87	22.45	21.63
States with per capita incomes of:					
Less than $1,400	a	17.42	19.03	a	a
More than $1,400	a	a	20.71	22.47	21.63
	Average Earnings				
All states	$47.04	$41.34	$45.94	$41.50	$42.36
States with per capita incomes of:					
Less than $1,400	a	41.34	42.09	a	a
More than $1,400	a	a	49.79	41.40	42.36

a No averages are given when there are less than two states in a cell.
Source: *Census of Business, 1948,* Bureau of the Census, Vol. VII, Table
101A; "State Income Payments in 1948," *Survey of Current Business,* Dept.
of Commerce, August 1949, Table 8; and *Statistical Abstract of the United
States,* Bureau of the Census, 1952, Tables 10 and 19.

would expect relatively fewer barbers with relatively higher earnings in states with longer periods of apprenticeship. No such
effect is yet noticeable.

It is possible, however, that the increasing barriers to entry into
barbering have had effects which escape our crude measures. Between 1939 and 1948 the average annual full-time earnings of a
barber increased from $877 to $2,160, or by 146 per cent, while
the average full-time earnings of all workers in the labor force rose
only 121 per cent.[20] Some such development as rising relative
wages seems necessary to explain the absolute decline in the number of barbers in a period when population and real income were
rising and no radical changes in technology took place.

[20] *Census of Business, 1939,* Vol. III, *Service Businesses,* Table 3A; the
figure is based on the number of full-time employees at work in the month
of November 1949. The *Census of Business, 1948,* Vol. VII, *Service Trade,*
Table 16, figure is based on number of paid full-workweek employees at
work in the workweek ended nearest November 15, 1948; see *National Income Supplement, 1951, Survey of Current Business,* Table 26.

CHAPTER 6

THE PROFESSIONAL SERVICE INDUSTRIES

A century ago the professions were a fairly well-defined group: law, medicine, the clergy, military officers, and a few small groups such as college teachers. These were all occupations characterized by a long period of formal educational training, and they were substantially the only occupations which required such training. Correspondingly, they commanded prestige, and as a rule they probably also commanded relatively high earnings—the tradition of poverty of the minister and the professor notwithstanding.

The vast expansion of formal education, in the United States beyond all other countries, has permitted a great increase in the learned occupations. The accumulation of knowledge and the increasing specialization of labor have led to the development of many new occupations requiring such training. A very incomplete list of fairly broad occupations makes clear the extent to which formal education is now characteristic of numerous occupations (Table 38). The traditional professions still stand at the head of the list when ranked by formal training, but many other occupations are approaching them. Modern technology gives rise to a host of engineers and chemists, and modern governments demand trained teachers, social workers, administrators, etc. The traditional professions are now only the leading species of a large and growing genus.

Yet we shall restrict our discussion to four traditional professions. Some limitations are necessary, and these professions are still large, and—unlike many of the newer professions—their members are still organized as independent practitioners or are employees of nonprofit organizations.

1. Trends in Numbers

We cannot give a full account of each of the professions chosen to represent this group of industries. Instead, we shall first consider the trends in numbers employed, then the methods of recruitment and the forms of business organization, and finally the earnings.

NUMBERS IN THE PROFESSIONS

The decennial data on numbers in the four professions we have chosen for study are presented in Table 39, and in Chart 26 fuller

106

TABLE 38

College-Trained Persons as a Percentage
of All Members of Selected Occupations, 1940

	Number in Labor Force	Number with 4 or More Years of College	% in Labor Force with 4 or More Years of College
•llege presidents, professors, and instructors	75,760	71,020	93.74
ysicians and surgeons	164,760	152,980	92.85
wyers and judges	183,080	146,460	80.00
ntists, pharmacists, osteopaths, and veterinarians	173,240	106,900	61.71
ergymen	136,560	83,700	61.29
ectrical engineers	55,440	33,540	60.50
echanical engineers	82,920	49,120	59.24
vil engineers	86,140	51,000	59.21
her technical engineers	30,980	22,100	71.34
emists, assayers, and metallurgists	55,640	32,620	58.63
achers[a]	1,052,960	593,920	56.40
chitects	20,740	11,640	56.12
cial and welfare workers	73,880	38,320	51.87
orarians	33,320	15,240	45.74
thors, editors, and reporters	76,240	29,520	38.72
sicians and music teachers	149,900	31,120	20.76
signers and draftsmen	107,940	16,020	14.84

[a] Not including college professors and instructors.
Source: *Census of Population, 1940*, Bureau of the Census, *The Labor Force (Sample tistics), Occupational Characteristics*, Tables 1 and 3.

data from other sources are given. In addition, the numbers in dentistry and the ministry have been reported, although they are not included in our subsequent discussion.

The profession which has grown most rapidly in numbers is that of commissioned military officers. The growth in numbers from 4,000 in 1900 to 131,000 in 1950 is not due to the inclusion of years of active hostilities (see Chart 26)—in 1918 there were 214,000 officers and in 1945, 1,300,000 officers. Aside from periods of active hostilities, the number of officers tended to grow only slowly, but the average number rose to a new level after each war: it averaged 7,000 from 1900 to 1910, 25,000 from 1920 to 1940, and 188,000 in 1948-1950.

The basic reason for the growth of the military profession in this country hardly requires mention, but a second factor has also been

TABLE 39
Number of Persons in Selected Professions, 1900-1950

	Lawyers (1)	Physicians (2)	Dentists (3)	College Teachers[a] (4)	Clergymen (5)	Milite Office (6)
			A. Absolute Number			
1900	107,483	112,138	29,665	29,000	98,353	4,3
1910	114,704	134,195	39,997	45,000	118,018	7,4
1920	122,519	144,977	56,152	62,000	127,270	27,2
1930	160,605	153,803	71,055	105,400	148,848	24,8
1940	180,483	165,629	71,314	146,900	143,642	33,6
1950	181,226	192,317	75,025	246,700	168,419	188,3
			B. Number per 1,000 Population			
1900	1.41	1.47	.39	.38	1.22	.0
1910	1.24	1.45	.43	.49	1.28	.0
1920	1.15	1.36	.53	.58	1.20	.2
1930	1.30	1.24	.58	.86	1.21	.2
1940	1.37	1.26	.54	1.11	1.09	.2
1950	1.20	1.28	.50	1.64	1.12	.8

a Including academic employees in administration, full-time research, etc.

Column	Source
1, 3, 5	*1900-1940*: Alba M. Edwards, *Comparative Occupational Statistics for the Uni States, 1870 to 1940*, Bureau of the Census, 1943. *1950: Census of Populati 1950*, Bureau of the Census, Vol. II.
2	The number of physicians in 1900 was estimated by using the 1910 ratio of e mated physicians to total number of physicians, surgeons, osteopaths, and ot healers reported. The 1910 ratio was obtained by comparing physicians repor for that year by the American Medical Association (see *American Medical I tionary*, American Medical Association, 1950) with total number of physici surgeons, and osteopaths reported in the 1910 census of occupations. The num of physicians for the years 1920 to 1940 was obtained from Edwards (*op. ci* and that for 1950 from the *Census of Population, 1950*, Vol. II.
4	*Biennial Survey of Education in the United States*, Office of Education. For a disc sion of the large excess of Office of Education over census figures for college teach see George J. Stigler, *Employment and Compensation in Education*, National Bur of Economic Research, Occasional Paper 33, 1950.
6	*Statistical Abstract of the United States*, Bureau of the Census.

of some importance. In 1900 less than 1 out of 20 men on active duty was a commissioned officer; in the interwar decades and thereafter the proportion of officers has been about 1 in 10.

College teachers grew at a slower rate than military officers but increased by a larger absolute number during the half century. Americans outside the academic world are perhaps unacquainted with the prodigious extent of higher education in this country as compared with foreign nations. No other country has attempted to

CHART 26

Growth in Four Selected Professions, 1900-1950

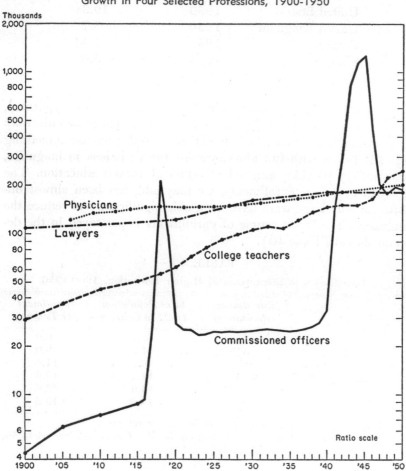

Source: *Physicians: American Medical Directory*, American Medical Association, 1950. *Lawyers*: Alba M. Edwards, *Comparative Occupation Statistics for the United States, 1870 to 1940*, Bureau of the Census, 1943, and *Census of Population, 1950*, Bureau of the Census, Vol. II, Part 1, Table 130. *Commissioned Officers: Statistical Abstract of the United States*, Dept. of Commerce. *College Teachers: Biennial Survey of Education in the United States*, Office of Education.

give a college education to so large a share of its population, as a few comparative figures indicate:[1]

Country	Year	College Students per 1,000 Population Aged 18 to 21
United States	1950	19.3[a]
United Kingdom	1950	3.7
France	1951	5.4
Sweden	1948	5.0

a The figure is 29.6 including veterans.

The extent of higher education in the United States is exaggerated, to be sure, by our practice of designating as a college or university almost any institution which is not beyond all pretense something else. Yet even with full allowance for the variations in language, our society provides unusual amounts of formal education. The growth of college enrollments, we may add, has been almost unbroken; only large wars have been able significantly to reduce the numbers. The broad course of enrollments is portrayed in the decennial data (Table 40).

TABLE 40

Enrollments in Institutions of Higher Education, 1900-1950

	Enrollments (thousands)	% of Population 18-21 in Colleges	Enrollment per Teacher
1900	238	4.0	9.0
1910	355	4.8	9.0
1920	598	8.1	11.4
1930	1,101	12.2	12.8
1940	1,494	15.6	12.6
1950	2,659	19.3[a]	13.6

a Excluding veterans; 29.6 per cent including veterans.
Source: *Biennial Survey of Education in the United States, 1948-50*, Office of Education, 1953, Chap. 4, Sec. 1, p. 6.

The growth in the number of lawyers has been relatively modest —68.6 per cent in the half century, or moderately less than the growth of population. Since the number of laws and regulations affecting each individual has presumably increased, and a vast host

[1] *Annuaire Statistique, 1951*, Paris, 1951, pp. 25 and 61; *Statistisk Årsbök, 1951*, Stockholm, 1951, pp. 8 and 94; *Annual Abstract of Statistics, 1952*, London, 1952, pp. 14 and 274 ff.; and *Biennial Survey of Education in the United States, 1948-50*, Office of Education, Chap. 4, Sec. 1, p. 6.

of government regulatory bodies have appeared in the half century, one would expect a considerably larger growth than has actually taken place. One may conjecture that two forces have served to reduce the growth of lawyers. The first is the progressive increase in the standards of professional training, which we discuss below. The second is the growth of specialization in the law. There probably has. been some increase in the degree of specialization in branches of the law (patent, antitrust, labor, etc.), with some increase in capacity to handle legal business. The lawyer of fifty years ago was also more inclined to blend a variety of business activities with his practice of law.

Our final profession, the physicians, has grown least rapidly, and the ratio of physicians to population has declined by 17 per cent from 1900 to 1950. The decline is largely the result of the vast rise in the quality and duration of medical training during the early decades of the century, a matter we shall discuss below. A second factor has been scientific progress: the past generation has witnessed one of the golden ages of medical progress, with advances in techniques, equipment, and medical preparations following so fast on one another as to invite analogy with the industrial revolution. This brilliant progress has been both a cause and an effect of progressive specialization by physicians, which probably serves to increase the number of patients one physician can care for—as well as the number of physicians one patient cares for.

2. Recruitment and Business Organization

LAW

A century ago the training of lawyers was still dominantly acquired by apprenticeship—by "reading" in a law office. Indeed, the trend toward elimination of requirements for legal training was then reaching an extreme: "Every citizen twenty-one years of age, in New Hampshire after 1842, every citizen of Maine after 1843, every resident of Wisconsin after 1849, and every voter in Indiana after 1851, was entitled to be admitted to practice in these states merely on proof of good moral character."[2] Even under these circumstances the professional nature of the bar was maintained by various devices, including ostracism of the nonqualified, and after the Civil War an increasing amount of training began to be prescribed for lawyers.

[2] A. Z. Reed, *Training for the Public Profession of the Law*, Carnegie Foundation, Bull. 15, 1921, pp. 87-88.

Law schools gradually developed during the nineteenth century —there were none at its beginning—until by 1894 there were 72 schools with 7,600 students. At that time the average term was two years, but ranged from ten months to three years, and some schools met for only twelve weeks a year. There were only negligible requirements for prelegal education. When the newly formed Association of American Law Schools required, in 1901, that its member institutions require a high school education of students, this requirement served to exclude numerous schools.[3]

The standards of entrance to the bar vary among states much more than standards in the field of medicine. The duration of required prelegal college education varies as follows:[4]

Years	States
None	5
2	31
3	9
4	3

Moreover, twenty-one states still allow the candidate to obtain his entire legal training by apprenticeship (for a period of at least three to four years), although a majority require three years of study in a law school or an LL.B. This latter method of preparation is now almost universal: in 1951, of 178,700 reporting lawyers, 170,977 attended law school and 145,467 had a law degree.[5]

Exacting requirements for admission to the bar have always been opposed by the "John Marshall" or "Abraham Lincoln" argument: that some of our most illustrious legal and political figures would have been excluded from the law by the standards the reformers proposed. Evening schools still enrolled 35 per cent of the law students in 1952, and approval of a law school by the American Bar Association is not so important to the school as is the corresponding endorsement by the American Medical Association.

Partnerships have long been a popular form of organization of lawyers, but two and a half times as many lawyers are in practice as individuals (see Table 41). The dominance of the single-person

[3] See A. J. Harno, *Legal Education in the United States*, Bancroft-Whitney, 1953.

[4] See *Law Schools and Bar Admission Requirements in the United States*, *1952 Review of Legal Education*, published by the Section of Legal Education and Admissions to the Bar of the American Bar Association.

[5] See J. V. Martindale, E. J. Nofer, and W. Hildebrand, Jr., *The Second Statistical Report on the Lawyers of the United States*, American Bar Association, 1952.

firm suggests that specialization has not developed extensively in the practice of law. To the layman, at least, the complexity of the law of patents, or taxation, or admiralty, or antitrust, or other such fields would seem sufficient to foster and perhaps require extensive specialization, and of course specialization is not necessarily inconsistent with single-person firms. One explanation for the persistence

TABLE 41

Lawyers by Type of Employment, 1951

	Number	Per Cent
Independent practitioner		
Individual	120,340	53.6
Partnership	47,311	21.1
Salaried employees hired by:		
Independent practitioners	9,344	4.2
Governments (nonjudicial)	19,910	8.9
Judicial bodies	7,471	3.3
Other	12,997	5.8
Inactive or retired	6,974	3.1
Total	224,347	100.0

Source: J. V. Martindale, E. J. Nofer, and W. Hildebrand, Jr., *The Second Statistical Report of the Lawyers of the United States*, American Bar Association, 1952. A lawyer who is also, for example, a member of a legislature is listed both as an independent practitioner and as a governmental employee; there are 4,147 such multiple listings.

of the single-person firm may be that the mass of legal work still falls within a few categories, such as property transfers, incorporations, contracts, and the like.

MEDICINE

The training of physicians has been standardized and subjected to professional supervision to an unusual degree.[6] The medical schools are (with unimportant exception) approved by the American Medical Association (through its Council on Medical Education and Hospitals)—there were 72 such schools, plus 7 offering a two-year basic medical science program, in 1951/1952. Three years of premedical college training are required (four years in 8 schools), but 78.4 per cent of the graduates in 1952 had baccalau-

[6] See D. G. Anderson, F. R. Manlove, and A. Tipner, "Medical Education in the United States and Canada," *Journal of the American Medical Association*, September 13, 1952, pp. 99 ff.

reate degrees. The four-year course is succeeded by at least one year of internship. The full period of college and graduate training is therefore at least eight, and usually nine, years.

The training of physicians has undergone a revolution since 1900, when there were 160 medical schools with variable, but in many cases extremely low, standards of instruction. The American Medical Association took the lead in raising the standard of medical instruction, and since high standards have high costs, half the medical schools were eliminated (see Table 42). The powers of the Association were vastly augmented when its approval of a medi-

TABLE 42
Medical Schools and Their Graduates, 1900-1952

| | ALL SCHOOLS | | SCHOOLS APPROVED BY A.M.A. | |
	Schools	*Graduates*	*Schools*	*Graduates*
1900	160	5,214		
1905	160	5,600		
1910	131	4,440	66	3,165
1915	96	3,536	67	2,629
1920	85	3,047	70	2,680
1925	80	3,974	71	3,842
1930			76	4,565
1935			77	5,101
1940			77	5,097
1945			77	5,136
1950			79	5,553
1952			79	6,080

Source: *Factual Data on Medical Economics*, American Medical Association, 1939, and "52nd Annual Report on Medical Education in the United States and Canada," *Journal of the American Medical Association*, September 13, 1952.

cal school came to be required in most states before graduates could be examined for a license.

The original objective of the profession was to raise the level of medical training; in the 1930's it appears to have been supplemented by a desire to limit numbers.[7] The high earnings and prestige of the physicians have attracted many applicants, of whom only roughly half succeed in entering medical schools. The number of graduates was virtually stable from 1934 to 1944, but since

[7] See Milton Friedman and Simon Kuznets, *Income from Independent Professional Practice*, National Bureau of Economic Research, 1945, pp. 12 ff.

the war the number has increased by a fifth, and will presumably continue to rise as the number of medical schools rises. In 1952/-1953, 42 per cent of those applying for the first time to a medical school were accepted; and 30 per cent of those applying who had previously been unsuccessful were accepted.

Any intent to restrict numbers has been overshadowed in recent years by the financial plight of the medical schools, 63 of which are affiliated with universities.[8] Medical education costs four to eight times as much per student as the other branches of university instruction, but tuition rates are usually the same or only slightly higher.[9] Unless tuition rates are radically increased, or increased government financial assistance is given to medical schools—and both policies are opposed by the American Medical Association—the number of medical students will not increase rapidly.

Medical practice continues to be organized chiefly in firms containing only one practitioner (see Table 43). Yet it is probable

TABLE 43

Distribution of Physicians by Type of Organization, 1949

	Per Cent of Physicians
Independent	
Individual	66.7
Partnership	11.0
Employed by:	
Independent physicians	4.4
Government bodies and hospitals	14.3
Nonprofit bodies	1.6
Industrial concerns	2.2
Total	100.2

Source: William Weinfeld, "Income of Physicians, 1929-1949," *Survey of Current Business*, July 1951, p. 13.

that the individual practitioner has been losing ground relative to both partnerships and salaried employment, and will continue to do so. The growth of welfare functions of government has led to a continuous expansion of employment of physicians in hospitals and in other government activities. The growth of specialization of

[8] See J. D. Millett, *Financing Higher Education in the United States*, Oxford, 1953, pp. 178-189.

[9] In 1952/1953, average expenditures per medical student were almost $4,000; those for all college students, roughly $750.

physicians, which is due to the great recent accumulation of medical knowledge and the increasing urbanization of the population, fosters group practice (partnerships). In 1949, 46 per cent of physicians were full specialists (only 26 per cent were in 1929) and another 16 per cent were partly specialized. Even in the absence of a radical reorganization of medical practice such as has occurred in Great Britain, these forces will probably continue to favor group and hired practice relative to the traditional individual practitioner.

COLLEGE TEACHERS

The training of college teachers is more varied than that of the other professions we survey. Without important exception such teachers have a college degree and a large fraction have the master's degree. Only a minor fraction, however, obtain the Ph.D., although it is commonly employed as the standard of full academic preparation. This degree requires a minimum of 2 years of postgraduate training plus the writing of a dissertation; in practice it is seldom received in less than 5 years, and on average in perhaps 8 to 10 years, after the bachelor's degree. The output of Ph.D.'s has fallen far short of the number of college teachers:[10]

Decade	Increase in No. of College Teachers	Approximate No. of Ph.D.'s Conferred
1900-1910	13,000	3,750
1910-1920	13,000	4,700
1920-1930	33,700	12,800
1930-1940	32,200	26,600
1940-1950	72,000	37,200

Since many holders of the doctor's degree work outside the academic field, it is apparent that much less than half of the college teachers have this degree. It is more commonly demanded in the larger and more prosperous institutions.[11] Teachers with this degree have an average of about 7 or 8 years of college and post-

[10] 1900 to 1940: George J. Stigler, *Employment and Compensation in Education*, NBER, Occasional Paper 33, 1950, pp. 29 and 37. 1940 to 1950: *Biennial Survey of Education in the United States, 1948-50*, Chap. 4, Sec. I, Tables 1 and 4, pp. 40 and 50. Approximate number of Ph.D.'s estimated by interpolation.

[11] See the illustrative analyses in Stigler, *op. cit.*, p. 36.

graduate instruction; the profession as a whole averages perhaps 6 years.

College teachers specialize to a degree that is unique among the professions. Even in the smaller colleges a teacher seldom works in two departments of instruction. In the larger universities, and especially in graduate instruction, the specialization goes to great lengths: the work of one professor of mathematics or economics may be incomprehensible to another—although incomprehensibility is not always due to specialization. There are no general practitioners in college teaching.

If college teaching were not a rapidly growing field, this specialization would create serious problems. The changing demands for education sometimes call for relatively rapid changes in the composition of faculties. Since few teachers can shift among departments, the flexibility has been attained by differential rates of growth of the faculties. The number of college teachers has at least doubled every twenty years, so a given branch of instruction could shrink relative to the total by half within twenty years even if the absolute number of teachers were maintained.

The employers of college teachers are some 1,851 institutions (in 1950), of which 1,109 were universities, colleges, and technical schools—the remainder being teachers' colleges and junior colleges. The colleges and universities employ 86 per cent of the total professional staff of 246,700 (in 1950). Among the colleges and universities (to which we will restrict our discussion), 948 were privately controlled and 161 publicly controlled. Since aggregate enrollments in private schools were only one-fourth greater than in public schools, the average public institution is more than four times as large as the average private institution.

The private institutions collect more than half their income from students; the public institutions only one-fifth (see Table 44). Since private institutions spend somewhat more per student than public institutions,[12] student charges are more than two times as high in the former institutions. An economist is tempted to argue that one part of a competitive industry cannot hold its share of the market if it charges more than another part, even though this situation has persisted for at least three decades! One offsetting factor has been that private institutions are more often in large urban centers and therefore attract both local students and distant

[12] Millett, *op. cit.*, p. 113.

TABLE 44

Percentage Composition of Educational and General Income of
Colleges, Universities, and Technical Schools, 1950

Source of Income	Public Institutions	Private Institutions
Student fees		
Students	9.9	33.2
Federal govt. (veterans)	12.8	21.2
Governments		
Federal (except veterans)	14.8	12.0
State	46.3	3.4
Local	3.3	.1
Endowment earnings	1.1	10.6
Private benefactions	2.4	11.4
Sales and services	7.8	5.8
Miscellaneous	1.6	2.3
Total	100.0	100.0

Source: *Biennial Survey of Education, 1948-1950*, Office of Education, 1953, Chap. 4, Sec. II, p. 16.

students who can get part-time employment near the institution.[13] Another offsetting factor has been the increase in tuition rates in public institutions relative to private institutions (see Chart 27). In 1900, public institutions charged nonresidents only one-sixth as much as private institutions charged, but now they charge more than half as much, and a lesser relative increase has taken place in fees charged resident students.[14]

[13] See the statistical analysis by R. H. Ostheimer, *Student Charges and Financing Higher Education*, Columbia University Press, 1953, pp. 94 ff.

[14] The revised data on tuition rates in the institutions covered by the series in Chart 27 for the years since 1948 are:

YEAR	STATE INSTITUTIONS		PRIVATE INSTITUTIONS	COST OF LIVING INDEX (1935-1939 = 100)
	Resident Students	*Nonresident Students*		
1948	106	320	526	167.0
1949	106	343	586	171.4
1950	107	343	616	167.5
1951	104	348	616	178.8
1952	109	353	662	189.1
1953	119	373	710	190.7

Note: Data for earlier years, and the identification of colleges, are given in George J. Stigler, *Employment and Compensation in Education*, National Bureau of Economic Research, Occasional Paper 33, 1950.

CHART 27

Average Annual Tuition Fees in Arts Colleges, 1900-1953

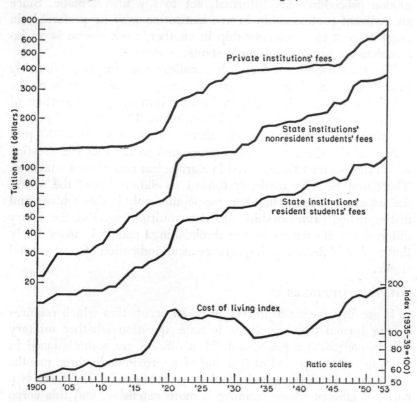

Source: *Tuition Fees*: Catalogues of state and private colleges (for list of institutions included see George J. Stigler, *Employment and Compensation in Education*, National Bureau of Economic Research, Occasional Paper 33, 1950, Table 21, p. 35).

Cost of Living Index: 1900-1913: Paul H. Douglas, *Real Wages in the United States 1890-1926*, Houghton Mifflin, 1930, p. 41. *1913-1953*: Bureau of Labor Statistics. Before 1915 the index is for the calendar year. Thereafter, the index opposite a given school year is for the preceding December, e.g. 100.7 was the index for December 1940.

The hierarchy of ranks in college teaching is fairly standard: instructor, assistant professor, associate professor, and professor. The latter two ranks are commonly permanent in tenure in the superior institutions, i.e. the associate or full professor can be discharged only for cause (neglect of duty, criminality, etc.). In 1952, in the land grant colleges 27 per cent of the staff were professors; 21 per cent, associate professors; 29 per cent, assistant professors; and 23 per cent, instructors. A few institutions have regular schedules for promotion (or discharge), but usually promotion procedures are informal, not to say unsystematic. Since an assistant professorship in one institution may be preferable in every respect to a professorship in another, rank per se is an incomplete measure of academic status.

The utilitarian basis for rank in college teaching is presumably that it offers a series of externally recognizable rewards to the salaried professional, useful in inciting him to the instruction of the young or the enlargement of knowledge. The growth of college teaching in the United States—there are probably 100,000 professors of the three ranks—has proceeded so far that the prestige which this scarce title achieved in Europe has now almost vanished. There may be some tendency toward an elaboration of the ranks: the associate professorship became popular only in this century and distinguished professorships are now multiplying. But the salary differentials among ranks are diminishing, and it is more likely that rank will decline in importance as an indication of professional status.

MILITARY OFFICERS

If one insists that a profession be an occupation which requires a long formal training, there is some question whether military officers constitute a profession. Most officers are commissioned in wartime, after a period of training of approximately three months —which is not always embarked upon voluntarily. Yet there is a corps of officers whose training is more extensive, and this corps dominates the profession. The two long-established official academies, West Point and Annapolis, each turn out about 700 officers per year, or a fraction of 1 per cent of the officers in the present armed forces. Yet these graduates constitute more than half the generals and more than four-fifths of the admirals (see Table 45). During wars their numbers are dwarfed by officers obtained from the National Guard, college officer training courses, and short-term officer training centers, and if the armed forces continue at present levels the academy graduates will be vastly outnumbered in peacetime also. But up to the present the official academies (and, to a lesser extent, a few private military academies) have been the basic source of professional military officers, and they are the only source we discuss.

The officer-candidate enters one of the official academies between

TABLE 45

Military Officers by Educational Institution from Which Graduated, 1950

RANK	TOTAL NUMBER	GRADUATES		
		West Point	*V.M.I.*	*Annapolis*
Army				
General of the Army	4	3	...	...
General	4	3	1	...
Lieutenant General	18	11	...	...
Major General	145	54	5	1
Brigadier General	199	116	1	1
Navy				
Fleet Admiral	3	...	...	3
Admiral	5	...	...	5
Vice Admiral	21	...	...	21
Rear Admiral	220	...	...	177
Air Force				
General	4	3	...	...
Lieutenant General	13	4	...	...
Major General	95	52	...	...
Brigadier General	135	69	...	...

Source: *Official Army Register*, Adjutant General's Office, 1951; *Register of Commissioned Officers*, Naval Personnel Bureau, 1951; and *Air Force Register*, Office of the Air Adjutant, 1951. (All January.)

the ages of seventeen and twenty-two—more often at the beginning of this age range—and undergoes four years of training. This training period is unusually short for a profession, and it is also unusual in that the candidate receives maintenance and $81.12 per month. The selection of candidates is primarily a matter of political prerogative, instituted perhaps less for its patronage value than because Congress has been unwilling to foster an undemocratic military officer corps. The appointments to the naval academy—those to West Point are broadly similar—are divided as follows:

160 (annually) are competitive among enlisted men in the Navy or Marine Corps.

160 (annually) are competitive among members of the Naval Reserve or Marine Corps Reserve.

2,650 (at any time) are chosen by members of Congress—five by each member. In many districts these appointments are made on a competitive basis.

75 (annually) are chosen by the President; these are given to sons of naval officers and enlisted men.

40 (annually) are competitive among sons of deceased officers or enlisted men of World Wars I and II.

In addition there are small numbers of other groups, e.g. sons of winners of the Congressional Medal of Honor.

The candidates, if they meet the exacting physical and modest mental qualifications,[15] then embark upon a four-year course, after which they are commissioned as ensigns (or second lieutenants, in the case of the Army and Marine Corps). The instruction at the military academies is provided chiefly by military officers assigned for a tour of duty to this task, and the military craft is therefore unusual in that it is the only profession of any size whose members are not trained by specialists. The illustrative tabulations for West Point (see Table 46) suggest that both the extent of

TABLE 46

Faculty Degrees and Experience,
United States Military Academy, 1953

	DEPARTMENT OF INSTRUCTION			
	Physics	*Mathematics*	*Chemistry*	*Social Sciences*
B.S.	3	15	4	3
M.A.	11	17	7	25
Ph.D., Ed.D., Sc.D.	0	3	1	3
Period of instruction at West Point (years)	5.2	3.6	3.7	3.2

Source: *Catalogue of the United States Military Academy, 1952-1953,* pp. 117-135.

training and the period of teaching are very short for instruction at the college level.

The avoidance of specialism, however, is deeply imbedded in the entire military profession. The statutes governing appointments and promotions make a sharp distinction between officers capable of limited duty and those capable of general duty, and place restrictions on the number and functions of those in the former group.

Promotion is governed primarily by seniority, modified by the power of officer-constituted boards to pass over candidates deemed

[15] The mental examination is waived if the candidate has successfully completed one year of college work.

unworthy of promotion.[16] If an individual is passed over twice, he is retired. In the Navy, for example, there is a period of minimum and normal service in each rank after three years' service as ensign:

RANK	MINIMUM SERVICE (years)	NORMAL SERVICE In Rank (years)	NORMAL SERVICE Total (years)
Lieutenant junior grade	2	3	6
Lieutenant	4	6	12
Lieutenant Commander	4	6	18
Commander	5	7	25
Captain	3	5	30

There are also maximum periods: a captain cannot have more than 31 years' service; a commander, 26 years'; and a lieutenant commander, 20 years'. If an officer is retired in the senior ranks, he receives a pension equal to 2½ per cent of his final salary times his years of service, up to a maximum of 75 per cent of his final salary.[17] If at any time an officer is retired for physical incapacity, he receives a pension of 75 per cent of his final salary. If he has been cited for performance of duty in combat, he is promoted one rank at the time of retirement. The provisions in the Army are similar, but put greater emphasis upon seniority and are less specific with respect to normal periods of service.

The distribution of officers by rank is also governed by general statute, more closely in the case of the Navy than for the Army. In peacetime the commissioned officers of the Navy are to be:

Per Cent	Rank
.75	Rear admirals
6.0	Captains
12.0	Commanders
18.0	Lieutenant commanders
24.75	Lieutenants
38.5	Lieutenants (junior grade) and ensigns

The Army has corresponding limits on the percentages of various ranks in the promotion lists, for example, 8 per cent colonels, 19 per cent majors. The actual distribution of ranks does not accord

[16] See *Officer Personnel Act of 1947*, Public Law 381, 80th Cong., 1st sess.

[17] Lieutenants of both grades, if retired, receive 2 months' pay for each year of service up to 12 years.

with these prescriptions, which are long-term peacetime goals, as can be seen from Table 47.

TABLE 47

Active Military Officers by Rank, 1949

	Army	Navy	Marine Corps	Air Force
General of the Army; Fleet Admiral	3	3	0	0
General; Admiral	5	5	1	4
Lt. General; Vice Admiral	20	22	2	12
Major General; Rear Admiral (upper half)	143	115	15	84
Brigadier General; Rear Admiral	177	120	26	107
Colonel; Captain	3,100	2,565	257	1,894
Lt. Colonel; Commander	8,362	4,592	678	3,760
Major; Lt. Commander	11,349	6,589	963	7,054
Captain; Lieutenant	21,564	10,118	1,530	18,900
First Lieutenant; Lieutenant j.g.	22,704	13,807	1,962	21,050
Second Lieutenant; Ensign	6,033	6,142	904	2,908

Source: *Second Report of the Secretary of Defense*, Dept. of Defense, 1949, Exhibit 8.

3. Professional Income

Each profession has a structure of earnings or salaries that is elaborate, and as a rule complicated—the exception is military officers, where the existence of a single employer, and of odd personality, makes for a greatly simplified salary structure. Professional earnings usually vary with extent of professional training, size of community, and age; we discuss these factors below.

In each profession, however, more or less peculiar forces are also at work in the salary structure. In college teaching, for example, the extent of the individual's publications influences his reputation and the frequency with which he is asked to teach at another institution. In a recent study of three large Middle Western universities, it was found that a professor's annual salary increased by 49 cents for each page of publication.[18] In law, earnings are probably greater for those who acquired a practice from their

[18] F. S. Kristof, "A Statistical Analysis of Factors Influencing Individual Salaries in Three Institutions of Higher Learning," Columbia University doctoral dissertation, 1952, p. 154.

PROFESSIONAL SERVICE INDUSTRIES

fathers. We pass over the factors which create differences of earnings among individuals within the classes we distinguish.

AGE

The life pattern of earnings usually appears as follows: earnings start at a relatively low level, rise at a decreasing rate until a peak is reached, and then decline at an increasing rate. This pattern is found in the independent professions, but not in the salaried professions (see Chart 28). Earnings in the independent professions reach a peak somewhere between the ages of 45 and 55; the teachers and military officers receive increasing salaries substantially until retirement. (If one could take account of the outside earnings of college teachers, total earnings would probably show a decline after, say, age 60.)

The eventual decline of earnings is easily explained: the energy, health, and financial needs of a worker decline after a certain age. These factors surely work also in the salaried professions[19]—why do salaries continually rise? One may conjecture that the proximate explanation lies in the existence of a hierarchy of ranks. In a profession with ranks, demotion for age alone will not be tolerated by the profession, and rank must be positively correlated with income or it will not serve as an inducement to and reward for good work. Another possible explanation is that the independent worker has greater freedom to vary his working time.

To compare two professions with different life patterns of earnings, one should not simply compare average earnings. Lawyers and college teachers begin to earn money at about the same age, and there may be little difference in life expectancy. Yet lawyers reach a peak in earnings between 50 and 55, but college teachers' salaries rise to age 65. Both life patterns may be converted into present values (we use an interest rate of 4 per cent), and we find that of lawyers (in 1947) was $135,035 at age 25, and that of college teachers (in 1949, using Kristof's sample) was $99,655. The former exceeded the latter by 35.5 per cent, whereas the average income of a lawyer was $7,517 and that of a college teacher $4,984, and the former exceeded the latter by 50.8 per cent.[20] The earlier the peak earnings in a profession, or the higher the earnings

[19] The accumulation of skill and reputation may serve as partial offsets, but they too are operative in the independent professions.

[20] The average salary is also influenced by the age structure of the profession, which in fact is a source of the high mean income for lawyers. The unweighted average life incomes were $7,302 and $5,279.

CHART 28

Relation of Age to Income for Four Professions

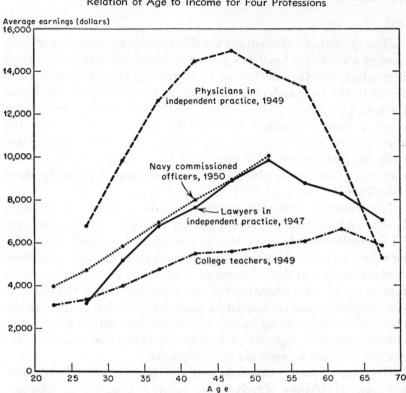

Average earnings (dollars)

Physicians in
independent practice, 1949

Navy commissioned
officers, 1950

Lawyers in
independent practice, 1947

College teachers, 1949

A g e

Source: William Weinfeld, "Income of Lawyers, 1929-1948," August 1949, Table 10, and "Income of Physicians, 1929-1949," July 1951, Table 8, both in *Survey of Current Business*, Dept. of Commerce; F. S. Kristof, *A Statistical Analysis of Factors Influencing Individual Salaries in Three Institutions of Higher Learning*, Columbia University Press, 1952, p. 40; and *Register of Commissioned Officers*, Naval Personnel Bureau, January 1, 1952.

in early years relative to later years, the greater will be the discounted value of future earnings.

SIZE OF COMMUNITY

In the independent professions, earnings are generally larger in the larger communities (see Table 48). The rise is consistent in law; in cities over 1,000,000, net earnings were almost three times as large as in communities under 1,000. These figures probably exaggerate substantially the influence of community size because

TABLE 48

Mean Net Income of Nonsalaried Physicians, 1949, and Lawyers in Independent Practice, 1947, by Size of Community

Size of Community (population)a	Mean Net Income of Nonsalaried Physiciansb	Mean Net Income of Lawyers in Independent Practicec
Under 1,000	$7,029	$3,694
1,000-2,500	8,775	4,708
2,500-5,000	11,297	5,060
5,000-10,000	11,581	5,516
10,000-25,000	12,282	6,350
25,000-50,000	12,903	6,236
50,000-100,000	12,991	8,501
100,000-250,000	13,083	7,332
250,000-500,000	14,368	8,348
500,000-1,000,000	12,877	10,057
1,000,000 and over	10,287	10,625

a Size of community for lawyers' distribution based on 1940 population; returns for physicians classified by size of place on the basis of preliminary 1950 census.

b Entire source of medical income from nonsalaried practice.

c Major source of legal income from independent practice.

Source: William Weinfeld, "Income of Physicians, 1929-1949," July 1951, Table 10, and Weinfeld, "Income of Lawyers, 1929-1948," August 1949, Table 8, both in *Survey of Current Business*, Dept. of Commerce.

there may be relatively more young practitioners in small cities, and specialists are chiefly in large cities.[21]

The earnings of physicians depart from this pattern in one respect: earnings decline after the city size exceeds 500,000. No persuasive explanation has been found for this phenomenon, which is not due merely to differences in extent of specialization or age.

In the salaried professions the effect of community size is less marked. Indeed size of community has no effect on salaries of military officers. No direct data are available on college teachers, but common observation suggests that salaries are higher in the larger cities and that outside earnings are a larger proportion of salaries in these cities.

PROFESSIONAL TRAINING

The only profession for which we have fairly extensive informa-

[21] In 1947, 47.9 per cent of gross earnings (aside from salaries) were received from businesses by the profession as a whole. See W. Weinfeld, "Income of Lawyers, 1929-1948," *Survey of Current Business*, Dept. of Commerce, August 1949.

tion on the relationship between training and earnings is that of physicians. In 1949 the fully specialized physicians earned almost twice as much as general practitioners; the respective averages were $15,014 and $8,835. The earlier analysis of Friedman and Kuznets suggests that half of this difference is due to the relative concentration of specialists in large cities and their greater average age.[22] In a study of three large universities, it was found that teachers with a Ph.D. average $878 per year more (in 1949) than those without the degree, holding age and volume of publication constant.[23] The preponderance of West Point and Annapolis graduates in the higher ranks suggests that graduates of these institutions also receive higher average salaries than other officers with comparable periods of service.

SALARY AND RANK

In the salaried professions, rank is the primary determinant of income. In military service the salary of an officer will also vary to some extent with the nature of his duties—flying and submarine officers receive extra payment—but this is a relatively minor source of variation. In college teaching, there is relatively little variation within ranks, and it is smaller the lower the rank:

SALARIES IN LAND GRANT

RANK	COLLEGES, 1950[a]			INTER-
	1st Quartile	*Median*	*3rd Quartile*	QUARTILE RATIO
Professor	5,299	6,132	7,037	.283
Associate Professor	4,351	4,930	5,492	.231
Assistant Professor	3,696	4,085	4,521	.202
Instructor	2,981	3,202	3,541	.175

[a] Teachers on nine-month basis.

There has been a noticeable tendency for the relative salary differentials among ranks to diminish (see Tables 49 and 50). In college teaching the differentials have decreased only since the 1930's, and may reflect only the primary need to make adjustments to the lowest-paid ranks during a substantial inflation.

[22] Friedman and Kuznets, *op. cit.*, p. 278.
[23] Kristof, *op. cit.*, p. 154.

TABLE 49

Salaries of Army Officers by Rank, 1929, 1949,
and Allowances

	CUMULATIVE SERVICE (YEARS)	SALARIES AND ALLOWANCES		PER CENT INCREASE, 1929 TO 1949
		1929	1949	
Major General	Over 30	$9,700	$13,761	41.9
Brigadier General	Over 30	7,500	12,222	63.0
Colonel	26-30	7,200	9,981	38.6
Lieutenant Colonel	18-22	6,638	8,271	24.6
Major	14-16	5,448	7,065	29.7
Captain	8-10	4,152[a]	5,859	41.1
First Lieutenant	4-6	3,252[b]	4,829	48.5
Second Lieutenant	Under 2	2,196	3,969	80.7

[a] Nine to twelve years of service.
[b] Three to six years of service.
Source: *Official Army Register*, Adjutant General's Office, 1930 and 1950.

TABLE 50

Median Salaries of Teachers in Land Grant Institutions by Rank,
1929, 1940, 1950 Salaries

	1929	1940	1950	Per Cent Increase, 1929 to 1950
Professor	$4,348	$4,245	$6,132	41.0
Associate Professor	3,359	3,272	4,930	46.8
Assistant Professor	2,691	2,605	4,085	51.8
Instructor	2,003	1,937	3,202	59.0

Source: *1929* and *1940*: George J. Stigler, *Employment and Compensation in Education*, National Bureau of Economic Research, Occasional Paper 33, 1950, Table 28, p. 42. *1950: Faculty Salaries in Land-Grant Colleges and Universities, 1949-1950*, Office of Education, Circular 283, June 1951, Table 3, p. 4.

MISCELLANEOUS FACTORS

We shall attempt no detailed comparison of the levels of income in the four professions, but certain other factors which would enter into such a comparison deserve brief comment.

1. Length of working year. The college teacher receives at least three months of vacation or—in the case of a third of these teachers —devotes half this time to summer school teaching and receives an approximately pro rata salary.

2. Pensions. Military officers receive 2½ per cent of their terminal salary for each year of service, up to a maximum of 75 per cent

of this salary. Thus 75 per cent of their terminal salary will normally be received after 30 years of service, or at the age of about 55. College institutions on the average contribute 5 per cent of a teacher's current salary to the purchase of annuities.

3. Outside earnings. These are unreported in the independent professions, but they are probably very small for physicians and possibly appreciable for lawyers. Military officers, one would assume, have only the royalties from memoirs. One may estimate that college teachers earn (aside from teaching in the summer) approximately one-tenth of their basic salary by outside work.

4. Perquisites. Military officers and their families receive a variety of perquisites such as free medical service and the privilege of purchasing through post exchange stores. Every profession has a variety of such perquisites, which we lack the information to estimate in terms of income.

5. Income tax. A progressive income tax will take a larger share of the income of a profession, given its average income, (a) the more unequally it is distributed, and (b) the greater the fluctuations of a practitioner's income through time. It has been roughly estimated that in 1941 the federal income tax took 14.0 per cent of the average income of lawyers, whose income is most unequally distributed (see below), and 10.8 per cent of the average income of physicians, and 2.7 per cent of the average income of college teachers.[24]

6. Duration of training. In order to offset the costs of training, the greatest of which is the delay in receiving income, certain professions require larger average incomes in order to be as remunerative as others. As a rough rule, earnings in a profession should be larger by 5 per cent for each additional year of training.[25] Military officers average about 4 years of training beyond the high school level, lawyers 6 years, college teachers 7 years, and physicians 8 to 9 years.

INEQUALITY

The independent professions display much greater inequality in earnings than the salaried professions (see Chart 29). The differences are marked even between independent and salaried physicians and lawyers. The independent lawyers, for example, probably vary more in skill and preparation than the salaried lawyers. Moreover,

[24] Stigler, *op. cit.*, p. 62.
[25] See Friedman and Kuznets, *op. cit.*, pp. 142 ff.

CHART 29

Lorenz Curves of Salaries of Physicians, Lawyers, Army Commissioned
Officers, and College Teachers in Land-Grant Institutions and
of Net Income of Independent Practitioners in Law,
Medicine, and Dentistry, 1947-1950

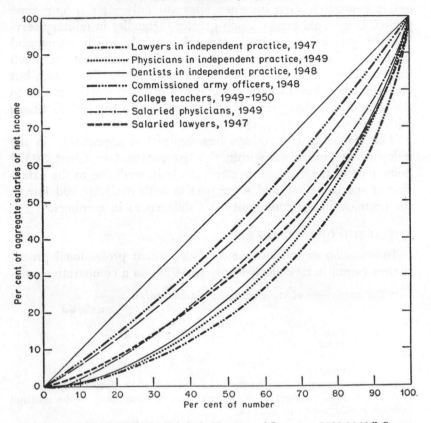

Source: *Lawyers*: William Weinfeld, "Income of Lawyers, 1929-1948," *Survey of Current Business*, Dept. of Commerce, August 1949, Table 5, p. 20. *Physicians*: William Weinfeld, "Income of Physicians, 1929-1949," *Survey of Current Business*, July 1951, Table 3, p. 13. *Dentists*: William Weinfeld, "Income of Dentists, 1929-1948," *Survey of Current Business*, January 1950, Table 4, p. 11. *Commissioned Army Officers*: *Official Army Register*, Adjutant General's Office, 1949. *College Teachers*: *Faculty Salaries in Land-Grant Colleges and Universities, 1949-1950*, Office of Education, Circular 283, June 1951, Table 3, p. 4.

the income of an independent worker will fluctuate more from year to year, so we should expect greater inequality simply because annual data are reported.

Much of the inequality within a profession can be explained by the directness of the rivalry between members of the profession (which is probably at a maximum in law) and the importance to the client of a slight superiority in ability (which is also often great in law, and is usually important in medical practice). College teaching has little direct rivalry, and superiority in teaching (although not in research) often becomes apparent only after a long time period. One would expect much greater inequality in military service than we observe: a great general is surely worth a thousand lieutenants, but great or not he receives about four times as much income. The perquisites of power are less equally distributed, but one may conjecture that the closeness of military salaries is due to the same forces that press all public salaries in the United States within a fairly narrow range.

The inequality of earnings has diminished appreciably in the independent professions within the last decade (see Chart 30).[26] Some part of the decrease is attributable in medicine to the extension of specialization, and some part in both medicine and law to the decrease in the community-size differences in earnings.[27]

THE TREND OF INCOMES

Information on the incomes of independent professional practitioners began to be collected only in 1929, so a comparative anal-

[26] The coefficients of variation tell a similar story:

Year	Nonsalaried Physicians	Nonsalaried Lawyers
	(per cent)	
1936		160.4
1945	96.6	115.5
1949	83.6	

Note: See *Survey of Current Business*, August 1949, July 1951.

[27] The ratio of earnings in the selected size of community to the national average earnings was as follows:

	COMMUNITY SIZE	
	250,000-500,000	*20,000-25,000*
Lawyers		
1941	113.5	82.4
1947	111.1	84.5
	100,000-500,000	*10,000-25,000*
Physicians		
1941	127.3	112.7
1949	121.0	102.5

Source: *1941*: Edward F. Denison, "Incomes in Selected Professions," *Survey of Current Business*, August 1943, Table 3, p. 24, and Edward F. Denison and Alvin Slater, "Incomes in Selected Professions," *Survey of Current Business*, September 1943, Table 3, p. 17. *1947*: W. Weinfeld, "Incomes of Lawyers, 1929-1948," *Survey of Current Business*, August 1949, Table 8, p. 22. *1949*: W. Weinfeld, "Income of Physicians, 1929-1949," *Survey of Current Business*, July 1951, Tables 6 and 7, pp. 14-15.

CHART 30

Lorenz Curves of Net Income of Nonsalaried Lawyers, 1941, 1947, and Nonsalaried Physicians, 1941, 1949

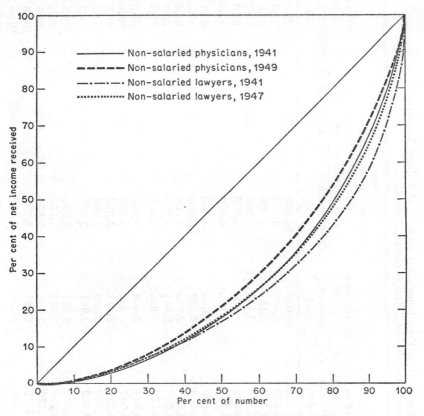

Source: Edward F. Denison, "Incomes in Selected Professions," *Survey of Current Business*, Dept. of Commerce, August 1943, Table 2, p. 24, and October 1943, Table 2, p. 17, and William Weinfeld, "Income of Lawyers, 1929-1948," August 1949, Table 10, and "Income of Physicians, 1929-1949," July 1951, Table 8, both in *Survey of Current Business*.

ysis of the trends of the four professions is limited to about two decades (see Table 51); the salaried professions are carried back two additional decades (see Chart 31). Salaries of military officers are changed only by infrequent acts of Congress—there was no change in salary rates between 1922 and 1942. Short-run changes in the average salary are therefore usually due only to changes in the composition by rank; the estimated average is given for selected years in Table 51. The salary of a given rank of college teacher in a given school also changes infrequently, but the large number of schools is an additional source of short-run variation.

TABLE 51

Earnings of Independent Practitioners and Salaries of College Teachers and Commissioned Army Officers, 1929-1952

| | AVERAGE NET INCOME OF INDEPENDENT PRACTITIONERS | | SALARIES OF COLLEGE TEACHERS | AVERAGE PAY AND ALLOWANCES[a] OF U.S. REGULAR ARMY COMMISSIONED OFFICERS | | COST-OF-LIVING INDEX |
	Lawyers (1)	Physicians (2)	(3)	(1941 weights) (4)	(current weights) (5)	(1947-49 = 100) (6)
1929	$5,534	$5,224	$3,056	$4,800	$4,232	73.3
1930	5,194	4,870	3,065	4,800		71.4
1931	5,090	4,178	3,134	4,800		65.0
1932	4,156	3,178	3,111	4,800	4,081	58.4
1933	3,868	2,948	n.a.	4,800		55.3
1934	4,218	3,382	n.a.	4,800		57.2
1935	4,272	3,695	2,666	4,800		58.7
1936	4,394	4,204	2,732	4,800		59.3
1937	4,483	4,285	2,843	4,800		61.4
1938	4,273	4,093	2,861	4,800		60.3
1939	4,391	4,229	n.a.	4,800		59.4
1940	4,507	4,441	2,906	4,800		59.9
1941	4,794	5,047	n.a.	4,800	4,800	62.9
1942	5,527	6,735	2,914	5,096		69.7
1943	5,945	8,370	3,039	5,096		74.0
1944	6,504	9,802	3,331	5,096		75.2
1945	6,861	10,975	3,277	5,096		76.9
1946	6,951	10,202	3,465	5,528		83.4
1947	7,437	10,726	3,736	5,528	6,081	95.5
1948	8,121	11,327	4,123	5,528		102.8
1949	8,083	11,744	4,234	6,552	7,246	101.8
1950	8,540	12,324	4,354	6,552		102.8
1951	8,730	13,432	n.a.	6,552		111.0

Notes to Table 51

a Including rental, subsistence, and money allowances.   n.a. = not available.

Source

Column

1   William Weinfeld, "Income of Lawyers, 1929-1948," *Survey of Current Business*, August 1949, Table I, p. 18.

2   William Weinfeld, "Income of Physicians, 1929-1949," *Survey of Current Business*, July 1951, Table I, p. 11.

3   Averages of median salaries from George J. Stigler, *Employment and Compensation in Education*, National Bureau of Economic Research, Occasional Paper 33, 1950, p. 44. *1940, 1942, 1950, and 1952*: Office of Education Circulars. *1943-1949*: Interpolated by expenditures on resident instruction per teacher.

4   Weighted averages of average annual earnings (computed according to specified years of cumulative service for each rank). Distribution of ranks for 1941 used as weights throughout (from rates of pay and allowance, *Official Army Register*, Adjutant General's Office, 1930, 1933, 1947, and 1950, and distribution of officers by rank, *Annual Report of the Secretary of the Army*, Dept. of the Army, 1941).

5   Averages for selected years obtained by using distribution of officers by rank of same year as weights except for 1947 and 1949, for which years 1948 weights were applied (from rates of pay and allowances, *Official Army Register*, and distribution of officers by rank, *Annual Report of the Secretary of the Army*, 1929, 1932, 1941; *Semi-Annual Report of the Secretary of the Army*, 1947-1948).

6   *Monthly Labor Review*, Dept. of Labor, September 1953, Table D-3, p. 1035.

CHART 31

Earnings of Independent Practitioners; Salaries of College Teachers and
Army Commissioned Officers and Cost of Living Index, 1908-1952

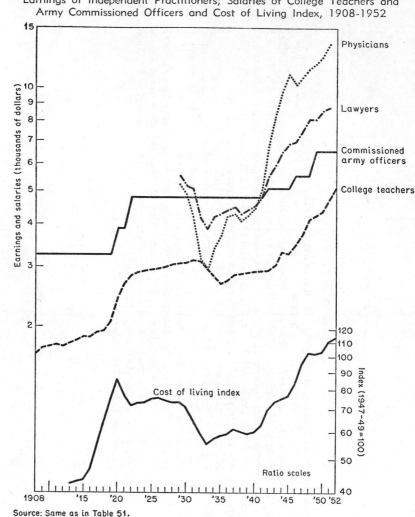

Source: Same as in Table 51.

The salaried professions differ strikingly from the independent
professions. The former fell relatively little during the 1930's—
indeed the rates of pay of persons of given ranks hardly fell at all.
On the other hand, earnings in the independent professions fell by
about two-fifths, and did not regain the 1929 level until 1942.
Thereafter the relationship was almost reversed: salaries of teachers and officers increased by one-half and one-third respectively

from 1940 to 1950, but earnings of physicians more than doubled and those of lawyers almost doubled. Lawyers' earnings increased much less than those of physicians, chiefly because with rising incomes the demand for medical service grew rapidly. If one averages decades, the difference between the two kinds of professions is emphasized:

	1931-1940	*1941-1950*	*Percentage Increase*
Lawyers	$4,365	$6,876	57.5
Physicians	3,863	9,725	151.7
College teachers	2,893	3,608	24.7
Army officers	4,800	5,487	14.3

There was a strong tendency for earnings of professional workers to diminish relative to those of the entire full-time labor force between 1929 and 1949 (see Table 52). The differential enjoyed

TABLE 52

Incomes in Selected Professions Relative to
General Labor Force, 1929 and 1949

	1929	1949
Earnings of all full-time employees	$1,421	$2,866
Lawyers	5,534	8,083
Physicians	5,224	11,474
College teachers	3,056	4,234
Army officers	4,232	7,246
Ratio to earnings of all employees		
Lawyers	3.89	2.82
Physicians	3.68	4.10
College teachers	2.15	1.48
Army officers	2.98	2.53

Source: *National Income Supplement, 1951, Survey of Current Business*, Dept. of Commerce, Table 26, p. 184.

by college teachers was more than halved, that of lawyers fell by a third, and that of military officers fell by one-fourth. Only the differential of physicians increased, proximately because of the great expansion in the demand for medical service with a lesser increase in the number of physicians. Two years separated by two decades are not sufficient to define trends, but it is probable that the differential between professional and nonprofessional incomes has long been falling and will continue to do so as a continually increasing fraction of the population receives advanced and technical educational training.

CHAPTER 7

THE BUSINESS SERVICES

THE industries that provide services to the business community do not form a category wholly distinct from those providing services to consumers; there is, indeed, a fairly continuous array of industries between the limits. At one extreme, service industries such as the consulting construction engineers serve only business; in the middle of the array, independent lawyers receive approximately equal shares of income from business and nonbusiness clients; and at the other extreme, teachers serve individuals in their nonbusiness capacity. Enough important industries fall in the category of those serving chiefly businesses, however, to justify separate discussion.

Let us seek some knowledge of the variety and nature of business services by means of an inventory. Our particular inventory is drawn chiefly from the classified telephone directory of New York City. It cannot pretend to be complete: many industries are too small in this city to support specialized business services, and many industries use other methods or media for advertising their existence. Nor can we be sure that all superficial differences in business activity have been eliminated. We have also deliberately omitted the largest of all business service industries—wholesale trade, in which specialization goes to great lengths (burlap, children's hats, hotel china, health foods, frog legs, pets)—in order to keep the inventory down to assimilable dimensions.

The inventory is listed in the appendix to this chapter. The most casual inspection will suggest the enormous variety and the extreme degree of specialization to be found in the business services. No commodity-producing enterprise grows large enough to be able to keep fully occupied the individuals who translate documents from obscure tongues, such as those employed by some small nations and most government price-fixers, or those who calculate the actuarial aspects of pension systems, or the lawyers who specialize in narrow branches of the law, or the individuals who plan bookkeeping systems or eradicate termites. Yet even the smaller enterprises use some of these services almost daily: legal aid is necessary to begin, to die—and to struggle along meanwhile; financial aid may be required continuously; a host of repair services are cheaper to hire when needed than to maintain.

138

It is highly probable that the reliance upon specialized business services has been increasing steadily over a long period of time. One cannot easily devise a measure which will record this trend: any inventory of business services at an earlier date, for example, would be different in length simply because of the changing practices in the classification of industries and the changing sources from which one derives his list of industries. Yet many of the industries listed in our inventory have arisen out of modern technological developments, or out of expanding government activities, and careful examination of business directories of half a century ago has revealed few lines of business which have since disappeared.

We shall survey the growth of employment in a few categories of business services for which data are available, and then discuss wholesale trade in more detail.

1. Employment Trends in the Business Service Industries

The vast detail of our partial inventory of the business services finds no counterpart in the recorded statistics: wholesale trade, the largest of these industries, was first enumerated in the industrial census of 1929, and the population census gives only the parsimonious detail on the business services reproduced in Table 53.

In addition we have information for a longer span on a group of industries—finance, insurance, and real estate—that serves both businesses and consumers (Table 54). Finance includes security and commodity markets as well as banking, and real estate includes both commercial and residential buildings; both are predominantly

TABLE 53

Labor Force in Selected Business Service Industries,
1930-1950

	EXPERIENCED LABOR FORCE		
	1950	*1940*	*1930*
Wholesale trade	2,042,072	1,294,001	
Advertising	117,183	79,035	70,246
Accounting, auditing, etc.	104,995 ⎱	161,452	
Miscellaneous business services	251,931 ⎰		
Engineering and architectural services	87,022		
Miscellaneous professional services	71,054		

Source: Alba M. Edwards, *Comparative Occupation Statistics for the United States, 1870-1940*, Bureau of the Census, 1943, Table 7, and *Census of Population, 1950*, Vol. II, Part 1, Table 130.

TABLE 54

The Labor Force in Finance, Insurance, and Real Estate,
1910-1950

	Banking and Finance	Insurance	Real Estate
1910	213,050	153,174	150,846
1920	390,952	225,783	177,997
1930	624,783	507,299	288,192
1930	605,953	512,357	351,591
1940	499,040	545,964	503,553
1950	626,187	770,095	552,697

Source: Daniel Carson, "Changes in the Industrial Composition of Manpower since the Civil War," *Studies in Income and Wealth, Volume Eleven,* National Bureau of Economic Research, 1949, p. 57, and *Census of Population, 1950,* Bureau of the Census, Vol. II, Part 1, Table 130.

The figures for 1910-1930 show the number of persons in finance, insurance, and real estate estimated on the basis of the census classification of these industries in 1910 and 1930; those for 1930-1950 give adjusted estimates for the 1930 figures so that they will be comparable with the 1940 figures for the respective industries. The adjustment takes account of differences in classification only (see Alba M. Edwards, *Comparative Occupation Statistics for the United States, 1870 to 1940,* Bureau of the Census, 1943, Table 7).

business services. Employment in each category at least tripled between 1910 and 1950, while the total labor force increased by only two-thirds. Despite this rapid upward trend in employment, the numbers in finance fell by a sixth during the 1930's, for this group of industries was unusually sensitive to the deflation and depression of that decade.

In the rapidly growing field of insurance, we do not have knowledge of the trend of employees by type of insurance, so we use premium income instead (Table 55). The primary part of the insurance business, in terms of income and no doubt also of employment,[1] has been life insurance, which serves chiefly nonbusiness clients. This branch has grown at a high rate relative to national product. In 1874-1883, premium income of life insurance companies was .79 per cent of net national product; by 1929-1938 it had grown to 5.85 per cent. By the recent period, 1946-1950,

[1] In 1935 there were 286,000 employees in home and branch offices of insurance companies, and of these 183,000, or almost two-thirds, were in life insurance companies. Presumably a similar distribution held for the 158,000 agents. See *Census of Business, 1935,* Bureau of the Census, *Insurance.*

TABLE 55
Premiums of Insurance Companies, 1869-1950
(*millions of dollars*)

			INSURANCE COMPANY PREMIUMS	
			CASUALTY, FIRE,	
	AVERAGE NET	LIFE	MARINE, ETC.	
PERIOD	NATIONAL PRODUCT	INSURANCE	*Stock*	*All*[a]
	(1)	(2)	(3)	(4)
1869-1878	$6,489	$83		
1879-1888	9,941	74		
1889-1898	11,671	199		
1899-1908	19,740	444	$278	
1909-1918	36,341	746	561	
1919-1928	72,160	2,081	1,479	
1929-1938	61,274	3,565	1,516	$1,781
1939-1948	153,349	4,955	2,592	3,227
(1946-1950)	211,867	7,027	4,317	5,429

[a] Stock and mutual companies.

Column   Source
1   *1869-1938*: Simon Kuznets, *National Product since 1869*, National
    Bureau of Economic Research, 1946, Table II-16. *1939-1950: Na-
    tional Income Supplement, 1951, Survey of Current Business*, Dept.
    of Commerce, Table 4.
2   *1869-1910*: Derived from *Spectator Life Insurance Year Book*.
    1911-1950: Life Insurance Fact Book, Institute of Life Insurance,
    1953, p. 46. To make the two series comparable the figures given
    in the *Spectator* were adjusted by the ratio of the estimates of life
    insurance premiums from both series for 1911.
3, 4   *1899-1949: Spectator Casualty and Surety Insurance Year Book*
    and *Spectator Fire and Marine Insurance Year Book*. The estimate
    for 1899-1908 was based on a nine-year average for 1900-1908 as
    no figures were available for 1899. There were no data available for
    casualty insurance premiums in 1912 and for casualty insurance,
    mutual companies, 1949. Estimates were computed for these years
    by straight-line interpolation. Beginning with 1950, *Spectator Year
    Book* no longer published separate volumes on Casualty and Fire and
    Marine Insurance, replacing them by one volume giving aggregate
    data covering all forms of insurance of this character.

the percentage had fallen to 3.32 per cent, but if one were to add
in all contributions to the federal old age and survivors' insurance
and the railroad retirement fund, there would be no drop.

To the 2.6 million persons in business services listed in Table
53, and perhaps half of the 2.0 million persons listed in Table 54,
one must add still a third large area of business services—those
supplied by governments. The services of government are sometimes rendered directly to business—as in the issuance of corporate

charters—and sometimes directly to consumers—as in education—but the vast majority of services (like highways and national defense) are rendered to both groups. One very crude estimate for 1936 indicated that 32 per cent of all government services were rendered to business.[2] Such a figure for 1950, assuming that government employment was roughly proportional to expenditure, would add still another 2.1 million persons to the business services. Even if one refuses to accept this arbitrary division of government activities, it is apparent that the business services are a substantial area of employment.

2. *Wholesale Trade*

The primary function of trade is to assemble and to distribute goods, without subjecting them to large physical alterations. This physical function entails or is facilitated by a variety of other functions: the collection and distribution of information, the extension of credit and the collection of debts, and the storage of commodities so as to reconcile rates of production and consumption.

If both parties to a trading transaction are businesses, it is wholesale trade; and if one party is a consumer, it is retail trade. But no such clear principle is adhered to in the collection of statistics: for example, the firms selling business supplies to farmers are listed as retailers—presumably because the number of customers and the size of the individual transaction are comparable to those in many retailing industries.

The basic functions of the wholesale trader may be performed by the producer or the retailer, so no sharp institutional boundaries can be drawn between these various groups. In 1939 the Census of Manufactures asked for the first time about the number of employees of manufacturing establishments engaged in "distribution," and found some 583,000 (out of 10,500,000) employees so engaged. Chain retail stores in that year had 60,800 employees in warehouses performing wholesale functions. If we could measure the employees engaged in wholesaling activities in mining, agriculture, etc., we should probably find that the total number of wholesaling employees outside wholesale trade establishments was at least half the number (1,700,000 in 1939) in wholesale establishments.

[2] R. W. Nelson and Donald Jackson, "Allocation of Benefits from Government Expenditures," *Studies in Income and Wealth, Volume Two*, National Bureau of Economic Research, 1938, p. 329.

THE GROWTH OF WHOLESALE TRADE

Our knowledge of employment in wholesale trade begins as recently as 1929.[3] The more than 50 per cent increase in numbers employed by 1948 indicates that wholesale trade has been absorbing a rising fraction of the labor force (see Table 56).

Trade has traditionally been regarded as a handmaiden to agriculture or manufactures, and less care has been taken in preserving its statistical integrity than has been taken in reporting

TABLE 56
Employment and Sales in Wholesale Trade, 1929-1948

Type of Wholesale Establishment	1929	1939	1948
1. Employees[a]			
Service and limited function	878,806	948,601	1,507,990
Manufacturers' sales branches	306,878	315,088	501,615
Agents and brokers	104,498	92,522	101,650
Assemblers	116,026	149,180	159,068
Petroleum bulk stations	79,016	99,956	112,466
Total	1,485,224	1,605,347	2,382,789
2. Proprietors[b]			
Service and limited function	n.a.	71,924	106,823
Manufacturers' sales branches	n.a.	385	781
Agents and brokers	n.a.	18,603	21,820
Assemblers	n.a.	19,493	10,114
Petroleum bulk stations	n.a.	23,061	23,952
Total	n.a.	133,466	163,490
3. Sales (in millions)			
Service and limited function	$29,205	$22,538	$79,767
Manufacturers' sales branches	16,175	14,254	52,739
Agents and brokers	14,517	11,779	34,610
Assemblers	4,452	2,510	10,958
Petroleum bulk stations	2,390	3,808	10,616
Total	$66,739	$54,889	$188,690

[a] Employment figures for 1939 and 1948 are given as of workweek ending nearest November 15.
[b] Number of proprietors for 1948 are as of November.
n.a. = not available.
Source: *Census of Distribution, 1930*, Bureau of the Census, Vol. II, Table 4, and *Census of Business, 1948*, Vol. IV, Table 1C.

[3] Retail and wholesale trade cannot be reliably separated in the population censuses.

"productive" activities—as is shown, indeed, by the fact that censuses of manufactures started many decades before those in distribution. As a result, the workers who were actually in wholesaling activities have only gradually been distinguished and separately reported. This type of growth of trade is of course a statistical mirage.[4]

The relative growth of wholesale trade has probably been under way for many decades, as part of the process of specialization of functions and organizations that permeates a growing economy. Business enterprises and industries grow so large that they find the organization of production a full-time work, and they delegate to subsidiary or separately organized enterprises the task of distributing the product among buyers.[5]

The growth of "vertical" specialization in manufactures and other commodity-producing industries would also increase wholesale trade. When a range of functions hitherto performed by one industry is divided among two or more, a class of specialists—the wholesalers—may intervene in the transactions. It is a debated question whether there has been any trend in the degree of vertical integration in American manufacturing.[6] If vertical disintegration has dominated on balance, as I believe, it has tended to increase the area of activity of wholesale trade.

[4] The instructions to enumerators in the censuses of manufactures of the period near the beginning of the century give some support to the view that wholesale employees were often included in manufacturing. For example, in the census of 1904 the special agents were told:

"Where manufacturing is incident to a mercantile business, the capital, employees, wages, etc. reported on the schedule must pertain only to manufacturing, but where the mercantile . . . is incident to the manufacturing, the report must cover the entire business. . . . the mercantile and manufacturing branches of the business being dependent upon each other, and the accounts are not separable, the report must cover the operations of the entire establishment. . . ." *Census of Manufactures, 1905*, Bureau of the Census, Part I, pars. 82 and 86, pp. 631-632.

Indeed, it is natural to expect that in a period when manufacturing was reported and wholesaling was not, the efforts at comprehensiveness would not be deterred by the fear of over-comprehensiveness, at least to the same extent as when wholesaling was also reported.

[5] For an elaboration of this argument with respect to underdeveloped economies, see P. T. Bauer and B. S. Yamey, "Economic Progress and Occupational Distribution," *Economic Journal*, December 1951, pp. 741-756.

[6] See M. A. Adelman, "Concept and Statistical Measurement of Vertical Integration," in *Business Concentration and Price Policy*, Princeton University Press for National Bureau of Economic Research, 1955, and G. Stigler, "The Division of Labor Is Limited by the Extent of the Market," *Journal of Political Economy*, June 1951, p. 185.

Barger's study of trade suggests that employment in distribution (retail and wholesale trade combined) grew three times as fast as employment in the commodity-producing industries (agriculture, manufactures, and mining) from 1869 to 1949.[7] The movement of all trade can differ substantially from that in wholesale trade, but for the reasons just given it is plausible to assume that employment in wholesale trade also grew relative to employment in the commodity-producing industries. Barger gives several explanations for this comparative trend of employment in "production" and "distribution." Hours fell somewhat more rapidly, and from a somewhat higher level, in trade than in the commodity-producing industries. The share of goods entering distribution has increased, a movement we have already commented upon.

Barger's chief explanation for the more rapid growth of employment in trade, however, is that productivity has increased less rapidly than in the commodity-producing industries. He estimates that output per man-hour grew 2.3 per cent a year in the latter industries, but only 1.0 per cent a year in wholesale-and-retail trade. If one defines productivity as output per unit of labor, the explanation is of course tautologically complete.

But if one defines productivity as output per unit of all inputs, then it is less certain that the growth of productivity in trade, and especially wholesale trade, has been so much slower than that in commodity-producing industries. These latter industries have economized in the use of labor but have been relatively prodigal in the use of capital. It is probable that in trade many of the basic developments of the economy have worked to reduce capital per unit of output.[8]

Inventories are the distinctive form of capital in trade. They will be smaller, the more rapid and economical the methods of transportation and communication, and the great advances in these methods have already been commented upon in Chapter 2. Inventories will also be smaller, the larger the market and the greater the volume of trade, because of the greater stability (of a statistical sort) in the rates of supply and demand. Thus inventories are in smaller ratio to sales in large cities than in small cities, despite the fact that

[7] Harold Barger, *Distribution's Place in the American Economy since 1869*, Princeton University Press for NBER, 1955, Table 14.

[8] See Barger's estimates of labor and nonlabor costs in trade; *ibid.*, Appendix Table A-3.

the variety of goods is greater in large cities. The economies in capital and/or improvement in service have probably been substantial.

THE FUNCTIONS OF THE WHOLESALER

Since the central task of the wholesaler is the assembly and distribution of goods, the importance of his work (measured by the ratio of costs to receipts) will vary with certain characteristics of the buyers and sellers and of the commodities in which he deals. One may suggest several relevant characteristics.

The first characteristic is the number of buyers and sellers with whom the wholesaler deals. The smaller the number—given the volume of sales—the less will be the costs of solicitation, information, closing of transactions, investigation of credit, etc. Therefore we should expect the operating cost ratio of wholesalers to be smaller when they are intermediaries between relatively small numbers of producers and buyers.

The second characteristic is the homogeneity of the commodities handled by the wholesaler. If he must assemble, not merely from many firms but also from many industries, or if he must sell, not merely to many firms but also to many industries, it is probable that his costs will be higher. It is more difficult to keep informed about, and canvass customers in, a series of different markets than to keep informed about, and canvass customers in, a single market.[9] There will be greater inventory requirements for given fluctuations in sales.

A third characteristic is the correspondence between the time patterns of production and consumption. The more complete this correspondence, the smaller will be the inventory requirements of finished goods. The correspondence is perfect, at one extreme, for made-to-order goods; it is almost perverse in the case of commodities (like used books and stamps) which are no longer produced.

A fourth characteristic is the economic durability of the commodities—the average loss of inventory values due to deterioration of commodities or their markets. Physically perishable commodities such as fish and baked goods and economically perishable ones such as stylish millinery will have high wholesaling costs.

A fifth characteristic is the range of supplementary functions undertaken by the wholesaler. Sometimes the wholesaler will install

[9] The cost of becoming informed on a market probably bears an inverse relationship to the size of that market, because specialist firms take over the provision of information in large industries.

or service complicated equipment (such as air conditioning equipment), sometimes he will engage in extensive advertising (as in the case of lumber); sometimes (as a sales agent or factor) he will advance capital to the producer.

Only one of these expectations can be translated into easily observed quantities, and that is the third, which asserts that operating costs will be in a higher ratio to sales if inventories are in a higher ratio to sales. It is confirmed by the 1948 data for wholesalers in forty different lines of consumer goods:[10]

Ratio of Annual Sales to Inventory	Average of Operating Expense Ratios (per cent)
2-8	15.8
8-14	14.3
14 and over	10.7

Unfortunately, none of these factors can be called to our assistance in analyzing the trend of employment in wholesaling, for we do not know the changes that have occurred in any of them. One may conjecture that there has been some decline in dealers' stocks because of improved transportation and communication. Conversely, however, the share of "styled" goods may have increased and that of made-to-order goods probably has declined, and these developments would be partly offsetting factors.

THE INDEPENDENT WHOLESALER

Whether wholesaling is undertaken by an independent establishment or by the manufacturer (or retailer) is not directly relevant to employment in wholesaling. Changes in ownership will not affect the nature of many functions undertaken by the wholesaler, and if a given change (say, forward integration by the manufacturer) eliminates some functions such as the manufacturer's selling effort, it normally creates other functions such as the coordination of diverse enterprises. Yet it would be an unusual coincidence if a large change in the role of the independent wholesaler did not have an effect upon employment in wholesaling.

[10] Ratios refer to establishments operated by merchant wholesalers in specific lines of businesses whenever these could be identified as dealing primarily in consumer goods—e.g. canned foods, flour, proprietary medicines, household furniture, etc. See *Census of Business, 1948*, Vol. IV, *Wholesale Trade*, Table 1E.

It is generally believed that the independent wholesaler has been losing ground to both manufacturers and large scale retailers throughout the present century. For the period before 1929, this impression rests chiefly upon various instances of the assumption of wholesaling functions by the manufacturer, and the rise of the large scale retailing units (particularly department and chain stores) that often buy directly from producers. From 1929 to 1948 the development is clearly recorded in the censuses of distribution: sales of manufacturers' branches rose 226 per cent while sales of independent wholesalers rose 173 per cent (in undeflated dollars).

It is evident from Table 56 that sales per employee are larger in manufacturers' sales branches than in independent wholesale establishments, and this is generally true also in individual industries. The difference cannot be interpreted as evidence of greater efficiency of manufacturers' branches because commonly—steel and cement are examples—manufacturers deal directly with large consumers of their products and deal through independent wholesalers in reaching small consumers. But Table 56 also indicates that sales per employee rose more rapidly from 1929 to 1948 in manufacturers' branches than in independent wholesale establishments. This trend may be influenced by a changing distribution of large and small customers of each industry between the two kinds of wholesale outlets, but it may also reflect differences in technical progress.[11]

The role of the independent wholesaler varies widely among industries: in 1939 he sold nine-tenths of the tobacco products and one-tenth of the women's clothing leaving factories. One possible reason for the decline of his role, therefore, is that those industries

[11] An analysis of the ratio of sales to employees by industry reveals that the changing composition of sales by industry had no effect. That is, in 17 industry categories the average ratio of sales per employee in manufacturers' branches to sales per employee in independent wholesale establishments was 1.7 in 1933. In 1948 it would have remained at 1.7 if industry composition alone had affected the ratio.

The 1933 data are the earliest available for individual industries, and with respect to employees they cover only full-time employees. To obtain an approximate estimate of total employees, full-time and part-time, employed in 1933, the number of full-time employees reported for each industry in 1933 was adjusted upward by the ratio of total employees to full-time employees in 1939 (see *Census of Business, 1939,* Vol. II, p. 17). The industries for which calculations were made are those reported in the *Census of Wholesale Distribution, 1933,* Table 3, and *Census of Business, 1948,* Vol. V, *Wholesale Trade,* Table 1E.

in which the manufacturer undertakes direct distribution have grown relative to those in which the independent wholesaler dominates. This is indeed the case, although to a very minor degree. One may calculate how the share of manufactures sold directly by producers would have varied from 1909 to 1947 if, in each industry, the share had remained at the level of 1939, i.e. if the changing composition of industry outputs alone were taken into account. For the large sample of industries for which this sort of calculation can be made, the percentage of distributed sales handled by manufacturers rose from 59.0 per cent in 1909 to 59.6 per cent in 1939 and thereafter increased slightly to 1947 (see Table 57). It is evident that the declining role of the independent wholesaler is due only in small part to the fact that he has concentrated in relatively slowly growing industries.

TABLE 57

Per Cent of Manufactures Wholesaled by Manufacturers, 1909-1947, Based on Assumption That Manufacturers' Share in Each Industry Was Constant at 1939 Level[a]

| | PER CENT WHOLESALED BY MANUFACTURERS | |
	Including Groceries and Automobiles	*Excluding Groceries and Automobiles*
1909	59.0	57.5
1929	60.7	60.7
1939	59.6	58.5
1947	...	60.7

[a] The share of manufactures wholesaled by manufacturers in 1939 consists of the per cent of manufacturers' distributed sales sold directly by manufacturers' establishments from the plant and through manufacturer-owned wholesale offices to retailers, industrial users, export-direct, and consumers. The estimate of sales wholesaled directly from the plant was obtained from Table 1 of the *Census of Business, 1939*, Vol. V, *Distribution of Manufacturers' Sales*. For the estimate of sales through the manufacturers' wholesale offices it was assumed that these sales were made in the same proportion as those made by manufacturers' sales branches and offices to their customers. The percentage distribution of sales by the latter agencies was derived from data presented in Table 7 of the *Census of Business, 1939*, Vol. II, *Wholesale Trade*. The two estimates were then totaled and the per cent of manufacturers' distributed sales wholesaled by manufacturers in 1939 was computed.

Note: The manufacturing industries included in these calculations accounted for 51 per cent of total distributed sales reported by manufacturing industries in 1939.

Source: *Census of Business, 1939*, Bureau of the Census, Vol. II, Table 7, and Vol. V, Table 1.

There is no shortage of explanations for the decline in the role of the independent wholesaler, and two of these explanations deserve some notice here. The first is that the manufacturers took over wholesaling functions with the development of nationally advertised brands. The independent wholesaler was unwilling to advertise any one brand to that producer's satisfaction. Once the manufacturer had taken over the difficult function of obtaining wide consumer acceptance for his branded commodities, he naturally took over the other wholesaling functions also. And as Kaldor says, "It is probably no exaggeration to say that without the support of large-scale advertising this attempt of manufacturers to release themselves from dependence on the wholesalers' goodwill, by building up consumers' goodwill, could not have succeeded."[12]

Because of limitations of data, all the hypotheses on historical trends in wholesaling must unfortunately be tested by comparisons of different industries at a given time. We may make such a cross-sectional test of whether advertising is related to the decline of the independent wholesaler. The Federal Trade Commission has complied the ratio of advertising expenditures to net sales for a considerable number of industries in 1940, and we may compare these ratios with the share of the produce wholesaled directly by the manufacturer (see Table 58). No relationship is evident.[13]

Another and more widely held explanation for the independent wholesaler's decline is that the mass retail distributors—chains and mail-order and department stores—have taken over the functions previously performed by the wholesaler, for each unit buys in quantities large enough to permit direct dealing with the manufacturer. A comparison of various kinds of retail business with the shares of manufacturers' output sold directly to independent wholesalers must be very approximate because neither the retail nor the wholesale kinds of business are homogeneous classes. But where at least rough comparisons can be made, again we find no apparent tendency for the independent wholesaler's share to be larger where the chain stores' share is smaller (see Table 59).

The limitations of cross-sectional studies in explaining historical

[12] "The Economic Aspects of Advertising," *Review of Economic Studies*, Vol. XXIII (1), No. 45, p. 18. See also J. B. Jeffreys, *Retail Trading in Britain, 1850-1950*, Cambridge University Press, 1954, p. 12.

[13] Nor is there any relationship evident when the ratio of advertising plus selling plus delivery costs to net sales is compared with the share of produce wholesaled by the producer.

TABLE 58

Per Cent of Selected Consumer Goods Distributed by Independent
Wholesalers and Advertising Expenditures as a Per
Cent of Manufacturers' Sales, 1939

Per Cent of Advertising Expenditures to Sales	Number of Industries	Average Per Cent Distributed by Independent Wholesalers
0 to 1.00	4	37.9
1.00 to 2.5	6	30.2
2.5 to 5.0	6	30.9
5.0 to 10.00	4	66.3
10.0 to 15.0	4	32.7
Total	24	

Source: Advertising expenditures from *Report of the Federal Trade Commission on Distribution Methods and Costs*, Federal Trade Commission, Part V, *Advertising as a Factor in Distribution*, 1944, Table 1. Other data from *Census of Business, 1939*, Bureau of the Census, Vol. V, *Manufacturers' Sales*.

TABLE 59

Shares of Retail Sales Made by Chain Stores and
Share of Goods Sold by Independent Wholesalers, 1939

Kind of Business	Per Cent of Retail Sales Made by Chain Stores (1)	Independent Wholesalers' Share as Per Cent of Goods Entering into Wholesale Distribution (2)
Farm machinery	4.9	10.0
Automotive (incl. tubes and tires)	6.8	51.9
Shoes	8.3	16.5
Jewelry	9.8	63.7
Optical goods	13.8	59.7
Hardware, paints, etc.	15.8	62.0
Lumber and construction material	19.8	44.3
Radios	29.5	67.7
Beer, wines, and liquors	32.0	75.3
Plumbing and heating equipment	34.2	51.0
Groceries and food	34.6	44.5
Furniture and house furnishings	37.1	31.1
Men's and boys' clothing	37.5	12.9
Books, newspapers, and periodicals	38.3	91.6
Women's and children's clothing	43.0	16.8
Drugs	44.9	62.4
Tobacco	49.8	90.1

Column	Source
1	*Census of Business, 1939*, Bureau of the Census, Vol. I, Part 1.
2	Based on sales of service and limited-function wholesalers made to retailers as a per cent of total sales made to retailers by service and limited-function wholesalers, manufacturers' sales offices, agents and brokers, assemblers, and manufacturers. *Census of Business, 1939*, Vol. II, Table 7, and Vol. V, Table 1.

trends, and the deficiencies even in the cross-sectional data, are sufficient bases for not rejecting out of hand either of the foregoing explanations. Indeed the directly observable assumption of wholesaling functions by the large scale retailers is sufficient to show that chain store growth has worked to some extent to reduce the work of the independent wholesaler.

Appendix
Business Services, New York City, 1953

ADVERTISING, PUBLICITY, AND SELLING[14]

Advertising Consultants
Advertising Agencies
Advertising
  Aerial
  Direct mail
  Outdoor
  Transportation
Advertising Artists
Auctioneers
Bookbinding, Catalogs
Catalog Preparation Service
Circulation Builders
Convention Services
Copy Writers
Displays
  Exposition, convention, counter, window
  Installation service
Display Consultants
Distributing Service, Samples, Circulars
Expositions

Fund-Raising Organizations
Graphic Designers
Hand Painting
Information Bureaus
News Service
Newspaper Feature Syndicate
Photographic Advertising
Photographic Color Transparencies
Photo-finishing
Premium Service
Press Clipping Bureaus
Press Photo Service
Public Opinion Analysts
Publicity Service Bureaus
Radio Audience Analysts
Sales Contest Organizers
Sales Organizations
Sales Presentations
Show Cards
Signs
  Painters
  Hangers
Subscription Agencies

GENERAL CONTROLS AND OPERATION

Actuaries
Adding and Calculating Machines, Rental
Addressing and Letter Service
Bookkeeping and Accounting Machines, Rental
Calculating Service
Charts
Circulation Auditors
Collection Systems
Commissary Contractors
Detective Service

Guards, watchmen
  Investigators
  Internal frauds
Dictating Machine Transcribing
Editorial Services
Employment Agencies Office
Farm Management Service
Fingerprint Experts
Handwriting Analysts
Handwriting and Typewriting, Document Examiners
Indexing Service

[14] Excluding all wholesaling services.

Inventory Work
Lie Detector Laboratories
Mailing Lists
Mimeographing
Multigraphing
Office and Desk Room Rental
   Service
Public Accountants
   Auditing systems
   Tax service
Sabotage Prevention Service

Shopping Service, Protective
Statistical Service
Stenographers
Stenotype Reporters
Tabulating Service
   Payrolls, sales analysis
   Punched cards tabulating service
Telephone Secretarial Service
Time Locks, Rental
Translators
Typing Service

INSURANCE AND REAL ESTATE

Appraisers
Aerial Survey
Building Management
Compensation Accident Service
Insurance Brokers
Insurance Companies
   Accident
   Automobile
   Burglary
   Casualty
   Fire
   Health
   Life

   Marine
   Plate glass
   Real estate
Insurance Inspection Bureaus
Insurance Rating Bureaus
Property Tax Matters
Real Estate Reports
Real Estate
   General
   Factories
   Commercial property
   Lofts, stores

LEGAL AND FINANCIAL

Banks
   Commercial
   Foreign
   National
   Savings
   Trust companies
Claim Adjusters
Collection Agencies
Commercial Paper, Discounting
Copyright Protection
Credit Adjusters
Credit Rating and Reporting
   Agencies
Credit Unions
Estate Management
Financing
   Accounts receivable
   Real estate, chattel mortgages,
     notes discounted, etc.
Financing Consultants
Investment Advisory Services
Investment Securities
Lawyers
   Admiralty law

Lawyers (cont.)
   Administrative law
   Advertising
   Antitrust
   Appellate work
   Aviation
   Automobile finance
   Banking
   Bankruptcy
   Bond—legal opinions on state,
     municipal, corporate, public
     authority
   Commercial
   Construction contracts
   Condemnation and certiorari
     Proceedings
   Consular law
   Copyrights
   Corporation
   Damage suits
   Employee profit-sharing and re-
     tirement plans
   Estates
     Decedent's estate

153

Lawyers (cont.)
Federal administrative law
Federal trade commission cases
Financial
Foreign law
Canadian
Consultant on Soviet law
European
Far Eastern
Italian and French matters
Latin American
Polish
Foreign patent licenses and information agreements
General practice
Government relations
Insurance
Accident
Fire
Health
Insurance claims
Life
Reinsurance
International law
Investment banking
Labor relations
Legislative and state departments
Medico-legal matters
Motion pictures
Municipal corporations
Municipal law
Music
Negotiable instruments
Patent

Lawyers (cont.)
Probate
Radio
Railroads
Real estate
Reorganization
Small-loan consumer credit law
Surety law
Surrogate's work
Taxation
Inheritance tax law
Franchise tax
Titles
Trade-Mark
Trade Union
Trusts
Pension trust
Unfair Competition Law
Utilities
Public utility law
Electric
Water power
Gas
Oil
Workmen's Compensation
Notary Public
Process Servers
Proxy Solicitors
Safe Deposit Companies
Savings and Loan Associations
Title Companies
Titles Searched
Trade-Mark Service

MAINTENANCE AND REPAIRS

Air Compressors, Repairing
Air Conditioning Systems, Cleaning
Aircraft Repairs and Service
Boilers, Cleaning and Repairing
Bronze Cleaning
Brush Cleaning
Building Cleaning Contractors
Cesspool Cleaners
Chimney Cleaners and Repairing
Coffee Urns, Repairing
Cooling Towers—Lining and Coating
Coppersmiths
Doors, Repairing
Electric Motors, Repairing
Elevator Shaft, Cleaning
Elevator Repairs and Installation
Engines, Repairing
Electric Fans, Repairing

Fire Violations Removed
Floors
Degreasing and cleaning
Waxing and polishing
Furnaces, Cleaning and Repairing
Incinerators, Repairing
Janitor Service
Machine Tools, Rebuilding and Repairing
Motion Picture Film, Inspecting and Cleaning
Motor Trucks, Repair and Services
Office Cleaning Service
Pipe Cleaning
Pumps, Repairing
Refrigeration Service
Safes, Opening and Repairing
Saws, Repairing

154

Sewers, Cleaning
Ship Repairs
Signs, Maintenance and Repair
Slide-Fasteners, Repairing
Steeplejacks
Store-Front Cleaning

Tool Resharpening and
  Reconditioning
Ventilating System, Cleaning
Welding
Wheels, Alignment Service
Window Cleaners
Window Repairs

RESEARCH AND PLANNING

Airport Construction Consultants
Architects
Business Counselors
Combustion and Heating Consultants
Communication Consultants
Construction Consultants
Designers
  Clothing, textile
  Showroom and office
  Structural, industrial, etc.
Engineers
  Acoustical
  Aeronautical
  Air conditioning
  Chemical
  Civil
  Electrical
  Gas and oil
  Hydraulic
  Marine
  Mechanical
  Metallurgical
  Mining
  Radio
  Refrigerating
  Safety
  Sanitary
  Structural
  Textile
  Tool
Estate Planning
Experimental Work
Export Counselors
Factory Locating Consultants
Fashion Stylists
Filing Consultants
Fire Protection Consultants
Genealogist Service
Hotel Consultants

Interior Decoration—Office
  Showroom
Labor Relations Consultants
Landscape Architect
Marine Consultants
Market Research and Analysis
Mathematical Research
Motion Picture Consultants
Package Development and Designing
Patent Development, Marketing, and
  Service
Plastics Research
Public Utility Consultants
Publishing Consultants
Reorganization Service
Restaurant Counselors
Sales Promotion Service
Shoe Stylists
Suggestion Systems
Surveyors
  Marine
  City
  Land
Television Program Surveys
Television Station Planning
Television Service Consulting
Testing Laboratories
  Chemical
  Containers
  Electrical
  Food
  Heat insulating materials
  Metallurgical
  Paper and pulp
  Paving and building materials
  Quality control
  Soil
Water Consultants

STORAGE

Fur Storage
Grain Elevators

Motion Picture Film Storage
Office Records

155

Oil
Warehouses
  Cold storage
  Field

Merchandise
Steel
Warehouse Representatives
Warehouses, Textile Specialists

TRANSPORTATION AND COMMUNICATION

Car-Leasing Lines
Custom House Broker
Custom House Broker, Air
  Freight Specialist
Freight
  Forwarding
  Domestic
  International
Freight Traffic Service
Messenger Service

Motor Truck, Rentals
Packaging Service
Packing and Crating Service
Publishers' Shipping Service
Ship Registers
Steamship Agencies
Stevedoring Contractors
Surveyor's Cargo
Trailer Rental Service, Commercial
Weighing

MISCELLANEOUS SERVICES

Appraisers, Jewelry
Assayers
Electric Meter Service
Employment Agencies
  Hotel
  Industrial
  Restaurant
  Technical
Exterminating and Fumigating
Maps—Mounting

Motion Picture Film Editings
Photographic—Commercial
  Fabric photographic decorating
  Industrial plant equipment
  Legal photography
  Liquor and beer licenses
  Photographic lettering
  Photo retouching
  Salesmen's photos
Recording Service

Source: All categories except lawyers: *Manhattan Classified Telephone Directory*, 1953. Lawyers: Martindale-Hubbel Law Directory, 1952.

CHAPTER 8

FACTORS IN THE TREND OF EMPLOYMENT
IN THE SERVICE INDUSTRIES

OUR survey of the trends in employment in the service industries has been devoted chiefly to individual industries with widely different characteristics. Their variety is of course the reason it was desirable to look beneath the portmanteau concept of "the service industries." Can we now, looking back over these industries, find major forces which have influenced most or all of them, and which would probably deserve special attention in studies of the many service industries we have not studied? This problem is the subject of this, our final chapter.

Every classification of economic forces yields categories that depend upon one another. Income, for example, depends in part upon resources, and both capital resources and labor resources (including number, quality, and training) depend upon past and present income. This interdependence is reduced, and our task of explanation is simplified, if we narrow our question: What forces govern the trend of employment in an industry which does not itself constitute any great share of the economic system? Then variables like income may be taken as at least approximately independent of the particular industry's fortunes, whereas, for the whole economy, income is determined by resources and technologies.

1. Technology

When one is concerned, as we are, with only the longer-term movements of employment, it is traditional to begin with or place special emphasis upon technology. Historical studies of manufacturing or transport industries seem quickly to drift into an exciting chronicle of unending technical advances. The emphasis has considerable basis: the machine or the chemical process often dominates the labor required per unit of product as well as the relative price and extent of sales of the commodity.

In the service industries it is easier to err in the opposite direction and minimize the role of technology. This is true because technological advance often takes two elusive forms. First, the advance may consist in an increase in the knowledge and skill of the worker, permitting him to work more rapidly or effectively. Second, the advance may take the form of an organizational change. Seldom, however, will technical advance in the service industries be so palpable as its counterpart in manufactures—say a loom or a hank of nylon.

Mechanization, to discuss first this form of advance, has been present. Certain kinds of machinery, such as electrical office equipment and elevators, are used by many industries (including service industries), but their ubiquity means that usually they have no preponderant effect upon the costs and prices of one industry relative to others. In a few service industries there has been an accumulation of technical advances of this sort which have had a noticeable influence upon employment trends. The retardation of growth and then the decline of the number of barbers, and more recently of beauty parlor workers, are attributable in considerable part to mechanical and chemical contrivances which permit the consumer to serve himself. The host of household appliances no doubt played some, although probably a minor, part in the decline of domestic service. Conversely, the changing technology of war is part of the explanation for the great rise in the number of military officers.

But in only one set of service industries—finance, insurance, and real estate—do we find relatively large amounts of capital per worker, and only in real estate relatively large amounts of durable, tangible capital.[1] In the other service categories, if an industry—like power laundries or cleaning and dyeing establishments—has special machinery complicated and extensive enough to be worthy of study, it is almost enough to classify it as a nonservice industry. It is worth noting that both of these industries have at times been enumerated in the census of manufactures.

The first form of technical advance we listed—increased skill of the worker—has probably had little direct influence upon employment as a rule. In medicine the advances have played a considerable part in preventing a rise in the ratio of physicians to population. This appears to be the only important case in our sample of industries, however. More often, increases in knowledge have increased the demand for services even more than they have increased the supply. If perchance present-day professors know more than their predecessors—as they should—it does not serve to reduce, but rather increases, the demand for their services.

The remaining form of technical advance—organizational

[1] Compare the last two columns in Table 5.

changes—is the most interesting. It is conventionally overshadowed by mechanical advances in the commodity-producing industries, but not so in services. We have found it to have appreciable importance in areas as different as trade and medicine.

A change in the organization of an industry is a change in the scale or range of operations of the business unit, or in the relationship among business units. In trade there were at least four changes in business practices worth recapitulating. The chain store took over some of the functions of wholesalers and jobbers, and on the other hand persuaded the consumer to undertake some retailing functions such as finance and delivery. The department store supplied to the consumer the convenience of accessibility to a wide range of commodities. The mail-order establishment persuaded the consumer to forgo certain services such as immediate availability and inspection of goods in exchange for lower prices. The division between producing and distributing has been obliterated for many goods as manufacturers have undertaken wholesaling, perhaps (we could find no wholly satisfactory explanation) in part because large scale producers and large scale retailers can dispense with the assembling and dispersing of goods fundamental to the wholesaler's function.

The economist is especially familiar with organizational changes, and it may be that he is prone to underestimate their influence relative to advances in natural science technology. The service industries remind us that such changes can have substantial influence upon the trend of employment, and suggest that they may also play a considerable role in the commodity-producing industries.

2. Specialization

Progressive specialization characterizes a growing economy. When goods are few and production processes simple, when technical knowledge is largely empirical and the pace of technology slow —then there is little need for specialization. But as goods multiply, processes of production become complex, technological knowledge becomes abstract and formal, and the rate of obsolescence of knowledge rises, specialization must become ever finer.

The business service industries are important beneficiaries of this specialization. The host of auxiliary enterprises that surround the commodity-producing industries embrace research, design and construction, marketing, advertising, legal and regulatory problems, internal control systems, training of specialized labor, and other business functions which require highly specialized knowledge and skills. The variety of these services and the small size of the enterprises supplying them together make for an incomplete enumeration of them by data-collecting bodies. One may plausibly argue that many are now misclassified in the commodity-producing industries and many are incompletely reported.

The consumer service industries have shared in this drift toward specialization. (One special change favorable to specialization, the urbanization of the population, is discussed later.) The trend is evident in the growth of specialization of medical practice, or in the proliferation of varieties of educational institutions. Specialization takes a different form when the family abandons activities, such as baking bread and even preparing meals, to business enterprises. There are reverse movements, as when technological developments returned much personal care (shaving and hair dressing) to the household, but the dominant tendency is in the other direction.

3. Income

The demonstrated importance of fluctuations in income in explaining short-run changes in savings and in the consumption of particular goods, and the obvious differences in the consumption patterns of rich and poor nations, give rise to the hope that changes in income will also be important in explaining trends in employment. The hope is not abundantly fulfilled.

Our experiments with income as a variable in explaining trends in industry outputs (and thus, in a more remote manner, trends in employment) have not been successful. In trade we found no correlation between changes in employment from 1920 to 1940 in the various states and changes in per capita income. Again there was no relationship between differences among states in the employment of domestic servants in 1940 and differences in average family income. A similar comparison by states of changes in per capita income and changes in college enrollments for the decade 1940 to 1950 displays an inverse relationship.[2] On the basis of budget data one would certainly have expected a positive association of family income and employment of domestic servants or college attendance.

It would be premature to conclude that long-term changes in in-

[2] R. H. Ostheimer, *Student Charges and Financing Higher Education*, Columbia University Press, 1953, p. 115.

come are a minor influence on consumption (and hence employment) changes. As a rule, income loses influence in these statistical studies only if other variables, which are related to income, are introduced. Ostheimer found that the educational level of the population was a very strong influence making for differences in college attendance.[3] High levels of education are both a cause and a consequence of high incomes.

Or, to use our own studies, urbanization proves to have a strong influence upon numerous service industries. Clearly urbanization is in part dependent upon income—the increase in urbanization in this country has been due most basically to the rising productivity in agriculture, transportation, and urban industries. Yet the relationship between income and urbanization is far from unique; many poorer nations are more highly urbanized than the United States.

Since we cannot isolate perfectly the net influence of urbanization (or of other characteristics we discuss later), it is possible that we have attributed some of the influence of income to urbanization or other variables.

And yet it would be timid to shrink away from the hypothesis that the absolute level of income is only a minor influence on the longer trends of consumption. We have observed in history poor nations that devote large shares of their resources to warfare or cathedrals, and can observe advanced nations that devote large shares of their resources to food and housing. It would seem plausible from daily observation that a richer person can better protect himself against possible adversities than a poorer person, but as our nation has grown wealthy the state has assumed an increasing share of the task of protecting individuals from economic hardship. It is easy to contrive or overemphasize paradoxes in this area. But it is also possible to overlook the versatility that societies display in spending a rising income.

The distribution of income among families may be an almost wholly independent source of influence on consumption. There is little enough knowledge of the size distribution of income in distant times and places, but what little there is offers no strong reason for believing that it is closely correlated with income levels. The trends of inequality and income level have moved inversely in this country in recent times. There are no doubt many subtle relation-

[3] *Ibid.*

161

ships between the two, but it seems that for considerable periods they may move rather independently.

The recency with which income distribution has been studied in a quantitative fashion, and the incompleteness of our present knowledge, make it difficult to determine its influence upon consumption and employment. We have used a measure of differences in the inequality of income among states to explain differences in the employment of servants, with fair success. More intuitive international comparisons point in the same direction. One may conjecture that the relative rise in the incomes of physicians, not paralleled in other professions, is also partly due to an expansion of demand for their services because of decreasing inequality of income distribution. It is too soon to claim that income distribution is a strong influence upon trends of employment, but it is probably not too soon to commend its use as a variable in the study of industries which sell much of their output to the wealthier classes.

4. Population Characteristics

The trade between urban and rural populations was a mainspring of the progress of opulence in Europe, according to Adam Smith. Their reciprocal needs, and the prodigality of landlords, were the bases for trade and accumulation. With his customary unvarnished prose, Smith wrote: "A revolution of the greatest importance to the public happiness, was in this manner brought about by two different orders of people, who had not the least intention to serve the public. To gratify the most childish vanity was the sole motive of the great proprietors. The merchants and artificers, much less ridiculous, acted merely from a view to their own interest, and in pursuit of their own pedlar principle of turning a penny wherever a penny was to be got. Neither of them had either knowledge or foresight of that great revolution which the folly of the one, and the industry of the other, was gradually bringing about."[4]

It would therefore be unhistorical to claim for modern times the discovery of the importance of differences between urban and rural consumers. But we may claim for recent times the beginnings of quantitative measures of the effect of urbanization and the demonstration that it can be an appreciable force even within periods as short as a generation.

[4] *The Wealth of Nations*, Modern Library, 1937, pp. 391-392.

In retail trade, for example, urbanization has brought a considerable amount of product, once produced and consumed within the household, into the money economy and into the channels of trade. In comparisons of changes in trade among the states from 1920 to 1940, urbanization displays a large influence, where income shows none. Employment in eating and drinking places has been growing very rapidly, and we find that this industry's customers are primarily urban dwellers. Urbanization has had similar effects upon routine service industries such as laundries and—to a lesser extent—upon professional services.

Compared with the differences between farm and nonfarm life, all other differences among communities of different sizes have relatively little influence upon an individual's spending habits. Since farm families have already fallen to less than one-fifth of the population, we may infer that changes in urbanization and community size will play a much smaller role in future changes in employment than they have in the past.

The age structure of the population also has considerable influence upon certain of the service industries. Enrollments in elementary and secondary schools are virtually in strict proportion to the corresponding population of ages five to eighteen. The strong upward trend in college attendance has served to diminish the effects of the fall of birth rates in the 1930's, but soon this trend will be reinforced by the rising population of college age, and vast increases in college enrollments are in prospect. We have also found that cities with a smaller number of children per family have relatively higher purchases of restaurant meals. The aged in the population are also increasing relatively, and this is a factor in the rising demand for medical service.

There are many other characteristics of our population that may exert an influence upon employment trends. The higher the percentage of married women in the labor force, the greater is the demand for some service industries such as beauty parlors and eating places. No doubt race and nativity and occupation leave their imprint on the family's habits. All we can say is that our unsystematic experiments with population variables other than urbanization and age have generally been unsuccessful in explaining changes in the rather broad categories with which we have been concerned.

163

5. *The Supply of Labor*

The composition of the labor force can also have a large influence upon the trend of employment in certain industries. In the great mass of semiskilled occupations there is sufficient industrial and occupational mobility so that any one industry, if it is not of great size, can recruit additional workers without encountering sharply rising wage rates. But at either end of the occupational ladder this is less apt to be true.

At the top of the ladder stand the professions (and the business executive class). The professions are by definition the occupations for which one requires extensive formal education, and we have found that over the past half century and longer the standards of training have been rising in every profession. Only because of the historically unprecedented scale on which higher education is supplied in this country have we been able simultaneously to increase both numbers and standards in the professions. Moreover, the expansion of numbers and the rise of training standards have been accompanied—at least over the recent decades for which we have data—by a reduction in the relative earnings of the professional classes.

Since the earnings of the professional classes still exceed the amount necessary as compensation for the additional costs of acquiring this education, one may expect a continuation of the growth of these classes. But of the traditional occupations—law, medicine and dentistry, clergy, military officers, and college teachers—only the last two have been growing rapidly. The primary growth of the professions is now taking place in engineering and business professions, neither of which is organized, as are the traditional professions, as independent proprietors or employees of nonprofit bodies.

Entrance into professions and occupations is increasingly subject to licensing requirements—we have encountered this development in medicine, in law, and among barber and beauty shop operatives, and we could have studied also elementary school teaching, accounting, and other fields. Sometimes the licensing requirements are designed solely to raise the level of competence in a field, and sometimes some desire to restrict numbers for ordinary monopolistic motives is present, but in either case the licensing may seriously affect numbers in a field.

At the other end of the occupational ladder from the professions stand the workers who lack both formal educational training and the skills that come from long experience. We find these workers preponderantly in the service industries—domestic service and routine workers in laundries, hotels, etc. In the past these occupations have been staffed chiefly by women, and especially by Negro and immigrant women. With the extension of education, and the sharp drop in the rate of immigration, this class of workers is becoming increasingly more expensive to their traditional employers.

Colin Clark's thesis that tertiary industries—roughly service industries—become an increasing share of the labor force as an economy progresses (as measured perhaps by rising per capita real income) is well known.[5] We saw in Chapter 1 that the American experience conforms to this rule.

Clark does not elucidate in detail the rationale of this trend, or the reasons why we find considerable variations among nations in the level and rate of growth of the service industries. The foregoing remarks provide a partial answer to these questions. We find that several developments which generally accompany economic growth in his sense do contribute to the rise of the service industries. The growth of urbanization, the spread of education, especially higher education, and the aging of the population—a consequence of falling birth rates and improving medical care—all lead to the expansion of important service industries. The increasing specialization that follows on expanding economic activity favors a host of business service industries.

But not all the forces normally accompanying economic development favor the service industries. The large decline in domestic service which is occurring in all industrial countries is also a product of the rising education and decreasing inequality of income, and the former development is surely and the latter possibly an accompaniment of rising real income. Technological changes cause the rise and fall of service industries just as they do of commodity-producing industries: the filling station replaces the stable when the automobile replaces the horse.

Moreover, these forces which we have found to be directly related to employment in the service industries are not in general perfectly, or indeed always highly, correlated with rising real income or any other index of economic development. We must there-

[5] *The Conditions of Economic Progress*, Macmillan, 1940, Chapter 10.

fore expect to find large national differences in the roles and rate of growth of the service industries: as between two countries with equal real incomes, the service industries will be larger, we may predict, the greater the urbanization, the higher the level of education, the lower the degree of inequality of income distribution, the larger the relative numbers of children and aged in the population, and so forth. Students of economic development may find it necessary to study a host of these phenomena, which are neither wholly independent of nor wholly dependent upon the general level of economic activity, before they can make tolerably precise predictions of the structure of industry.

It has often been remarked that research is an unusual form of purposeful activity: it sets out to answer questions but ends by multiplying questions. It is like a strange animal whose appetite is whetted in proportion to what it eats. We are therefore wholly traditional in our broadest conclusions: no simple rule describes the trend of employment in the promiscuous ensemble of service industries; a common group of forces seems to be operative in most of them; but we have not isolated all these forces or measured any of them very precisely. Responsible predictions of trends in this large area will not be possible until we have pushed much further in the study of individual industries.

INDEX OF AUTHORS

For topical guides, see table of contents and other front matter lists.

167

RECENT AND FORTHCOMING
PUBLICATIONS OF THE
NATIONAL BUREAU OF ECONOMIC RESEARCH

NATIONAL BUREAU BOOKS *are available from bookstores or Princeton University Press, Princeton, New Jersey, except that contributors and subscribers to the National Bureau should order directly from the Bureau.* OCCASIONAL PAPERS, TECHNICAL PAPERS, *and* ANNUAL REPORTS *are available from the National Bureau of Economic Research, 261 Madison Avenue, New York 16, New York.*

BOOKS

Patterns of Farm Financial Structure: A Cross-Section View of Economic and Physical Determinants	(in press)	
Donald C. Horton		
The Pattern of Financial Asset Ownership: Wisconsin Individuals, 1949 (1956)	196 pp.	$3.75
Thomas R. Atkinson		
Urban Mortgage Lending: Comparative Markets and Experience (1956)	212 pp.	4.00
J. E. Morton		
Personal Income during Business Cycles (1956)	208 pp.	4.00
Daniel Creamer		
Input-Output Analysis: An Appraisal (1955)	383 pp.	7.50
Studies in Income and Wealth, Volume Eighteen		
Short-Term Economic Forecasting (1955)	520 pp.	7.50
Studies in Income and Wealth, Volume Seventeen		
Minimum Price Fixing in the Bituminous Coal Industry (1955)	554 pp.	10.00
Waldo E. Fisher and Charles M. James		
Capital Formation and Economic Growth (1955)	691 pp.	12.00
Special Conference Series No. 6		
Business Concentration and Price Policy (1955)	524 pp.	9.00
Special Conference Series No. 5		
Long-Range Economic Projection (1954)	488 pp.	9.00
Studies in Income and Wealth, Volume Sixteen		
Mortgage Lending Experience in Agriculture (1954)	257 pp.	5.00
Lawrence A. Jones and David Durand		
The Frontiers of Economic Knowledge (1954)	376 pp.	5.00
Arthur F. Burns		
Regularization of Business Investment (1954)	539 pp.	8.00
Special Conference Series No. 4		
Shares of Upper Income Groups in Income and Savings (1953)	768 pp.	9.00
Simon Kuznets		
The Volume of Corporate Bond Financing since 1900 (1953)	464 pp.	7.50
W. Braddock Hickman		
Wesley Clair Mitchell: The Economic Scientist (1952)	398 pp.	4.00
Arthur F. Burns (ed.)		
A Study of Moneyflows in the United States (1952)	620 pp.	7.50
Morris A. Copeland		
The Trend of Government Activity in the United States since 1900 (1952)	288 pp.	4.00
Solomon Fabricant		
Federal Grants and the Business Cycle (1952)	136 pp.	2.00
James A. Maxwell		
Studies in Income and Wealth, Volume Fifteen (1952)	240 pp.	3.50
Eight papers on size distribution of income		
Conference on Research in Business Finance (1952)	360 pp.	5.00
Special Conference Series No. 3		
Deterioration in the Quality of Foreign Bonds Issued in the United States, 1920-1930 (1951)	112 pp.	2.00
Ilse Mintz